GOING GOING GOING GOING GOING GOING GOING

GONE GONE GONE GONE GONE GONE GONE GONE

going, going, gone!

GONE GONE GONE GONE GONE GONE GONE GONE

GOING GOING GOING GOING GOING GOING GOING

GONE GONE GONE GONE GONE GONE GONE GONE

GOING GOING GOING GOING GOING GOING GOING

GONE GONE GONE GONE GONE GONE GONE GONE

GONE GONE **by bellamy partridge**

GOING GOING GOING GOING GOING GOING GOING

GONE **illustrated by stephen voorhies** GONE

GOING GOING GOING GOING GOING GOING GOING

GONE GONE GONE GONE GONE GONE GONE GONE

GOING GOING GOING GOING GOING GOING GOING

GONE GONE GONE GONE GONE GONE GONE GONE

GOING GOING GOING GOING GOING GOING GOING

GONE GONE GONE GONE GONE GONE GONE GONE

E. P. DUTTON & CO., INC. GOING GOING

GONE **New York 1958** GONE GONE GONE GONE

GOING GOING GOING GOING GOING GOING GOING

GONE GONE GONE GONE GONE GONE GONE GONE

ACKNOWLEDGMENTS

I AM INDEBTED TO SO MANY FOR HELP, THOUGHTFUL CRITICISM, AND useful suggestions that I can never mention them all by name, especially the innumerable auctioneers who have submitted to hours of squirming before a tape recorder when they would much have preferred to be orating, or wheedling, or shouting at a crowd of bidders from the rostrum. I am particularly indebted to Colonel Marston E. Drake of New York for his information on the handling and selling of old and rare books; to Mr. Leslie A. Hyam for permission to quote from his charming editorials in the Bulletins of the Parke-Bernet Galleries; to Christie's and Sotheby's, both of London, for material about the history and prestige of their splendid London establishments; to Jimmie Leon, official United States auctioneer for the State of Connecticut, for his shrewd and penetrating comments on the use of fraud in auctioneering; to Mr. Ed Knight of Plainfield, Connecticut, for his colorful report on the auctioneering schools of the Midwest, and to Mr. Ed Beardsley for his description of how to sell country schoolhouses almost by the dozen.

I am also indebted to Mr. John D. Weaver of California for clippings about the goings-on among the stars at the Hollywood auctions, and to Dr. John Bakeless for the use of quaint records concerning the early book auctions in England. Then, too, I am indebted to Mr. V. J. Boor of the American Tobacco Company for books and pamphlets on the story of tobacco and the development of the tobacco chant.

It would be impossible for me to mention all the books consulted or quoted during the long period while this volume was in preparation, for they reached all the way from Babylon to the Book-of-the-Month Club. Some of these were helpful, some provocative, and some of them naturally of no help at all. I am grateful, however, for having had access to every one of them.

And finally I desire to express my extreme gratitude to the Library of Congress, the Yale University Library, the New York Historical Society, the Bennington Museum, the Library of Brown University, the Boston Public Library, and especially the Bridge-port Public Library where I am greatly indebted to the entire staff, and especially the Head Librarian, Mr. Julian Sohon, who made working there a real pleasure, and to Mrs. Clara B. Pearce, Curator of the Henry A. Bishop Historical Room, who gave me wonderful assistance in locating some of the most elusive material of bygone days.

CONTENTS

PREFACE

NOBODY KNOWS WHEN, WHERE, OR BY WHOM THE AUCTION WAS originally devised, but all are agreed that it was preceded by barter, and barter must have come soon after prehistoric man had acquired the idea of ownership. And after ownership all sorts of things must have begun to happen. Already man had acquired a money of sorts. In China it was small pieces of silk; in Tartary it was compressed cubes of tea; in Abyssinia it was salt; among the American Indians it was wampum made out of tiny pieces of shell; and in Virginia it was tobacco.

To exchange this kind of money for food or arrowheads or any other desired object came naturally, and when two or more persons wanted the same object and began to argue about it, the auction probably came into being. Reading and writing came to us from the Sumerians, but the auction received its first written notice in the *Chronicles* of Herodotus, the famous Greek historian, recording his visit to Babylon in the fifth century B.C. Herodotus mentions no name for this method of selling, but his use of the word "bid" would indicate some familiarity with the auction. A few centuries later we find the Roman soldiers disposing of their surplus spoils of battle to the highest bidder, a form of salesmanship to which they had given the name "auction" from their word *auctio* meaning increase. Later the French were calling it *vendue* and the Scots, with their customary economy, named it *roup*.

In all probability the word "auction" came to England with the Roman invasion and was brought to America by the early settlers. There weren't many things here to auction at first, but the custom was such a convenient method for the disposition of property that it persisted and throve until it became one of the greatest selling devices in a civilization built largely on the buying and selling of goods.

The auctioneer has his finger in every pie. Wherever there is anything to be sold, there he is, whether it is a truckload of food on the docks at daybreak, or the art of the world for the great auction galleries at night. Nothing is too large for him or too small. "What am I offered?" he cries, and the sale is under way.

I have tried here to tell the real story of the auctioneer in an informal and in no sense a definitive manner. With this purpose in mind, I have selected for this book the parts of the auction saga which have interested, amused, and entertained me most, hoping that readers will see them the same way.

B. P.

Easton, Conn.

1958

going, going, gone!

CHAPTER ONE

GREAT DAY IN THE MORNING

YOU KNEW AT A GLANCE THAT IT WAS EITHER AN AUCTION OR A murder. Nothing else could possibly have brought so many automobiles to so small a village. They were parked literally all over the place, big handsome cars of many colors from which people were descending and hurrying into Memorial Hall—or was it the Odd Fellows Hall? A harried trouper was telling people where to park, and now that the roadsides were filled he was admitting them to the parking lot behind the church for a fee of fifteen cents.

You pay your fifteen cents and try to put your car in the shade for it's a hot day, and as you shut off your motor you can hear a voice rather loud and oratorical in the distance, but you can't quite be sure what the speaker is saying. Then suddenly come the old familiar words, "Do I hear any more—are you all done—are you finished? I'm giving you fair warning, going once! Going twice! Third and last call—and sold to—what's the name please?"

You hurry your footsteps, squeeze your way through the crowd gathered around the door, and though you hate to be the pushing type you somehow manage to get down near the front hoping to find an empty seat. Not finding one you resign yourself to occupying standing room only until somebody goes out.

Glancing around you decide that it's a motley crowd. The front row is as usual occupied by the dealers and professionals, mostly men, with one or two sharp-eyed women among them, all of them brought there by the fact that some rare antiques had been advertised, and there might be a bargain lurking among them or an exciting bidding contest for a rare piece. Back of the professionals are the habitués who never miss an auction but seldom buy anything. One of them is calmly knitting on a sweater while her companion, wearing thick glasses, is bending over a small hoop doing needlepoint embroidery. They have come purely for amusement and wouldn't deny it if asked.

Nearly all the auctioneers have a few of these camp followers, especially the ambulatory vendue-masters who operate in a country area holding their auctions in one or another of several nearby towns. There are more of these habitués than one would imagine, some of them driving as far as fifty or sixty miles rather than miss a sale that promises to be interesting; and they have been known to stay at a hotel overnight so as to be on hand for the opening in the morning.

Back of the habitués come the general public, nearly all the women hatless, some of them in shorts, some in smart sports clothes, and a few queens in calico with blowsy hair, looking as if they had just laid aside a pancake turner. The women are in the majority, but there are plenty of men, most of them standing near the walls or leaning against pieces of furniture stacked around the edges of the room waiting to be sold.

While you are sizing up the crowd the auctioneer has sold a pair of Toby jugs, a cuckoo clock, and some odd pieces of glass. Then with a flourish he orders up from his helper a huge silver salver containing a complete tea set which he elevates after the manner of the sacred host, slowly swinging the salver in a semi-circle so all may see. Then with great care he sets the "equipage" as he calls it, on the table beside him and turns to the assemblage.

"Ladies and gentlemen," he says, his eyes kindling with promise, "we have here today such an opportunity as has seldom come to me in all the years I have been in auctioneering. As you all know, not a single piece of Sheffield plate has been made in more than a hundred years, and still I am able to offer you today this superb tea set including a teapot, sugar bowl, cream jug, spoon holder, and tea caddy with the original salver.

"You all realize of course that nothing gives a greater tone of elegance to a household than a noble tea service. This set has graced the sideboard of a single family for over a century, and so carefully has it been kept and treasured that not a dent or scratch can be found anywhere upon it."

As he pauses for effect a woman in the audience waves her hand to attract his attention. "May I ask a question?" she inquires.

He is obviously annoyed at the interruption, but replies stiffly, "It will be my pleasure to answer."

"Is this set solid silver—sterling, I mean?"

He throws up both his hands with obvious displeasure. "Great Day in the morning!" he exclaims. "Didn't I make it plain that this is *Sheffield plate?* Solid silver can be had any day in the week; factories are turning it out by the carload. Don't get the idea that Sheffield plate is a mere substitute for solid silver, for it's nothing of the sort. Sheffield plate is a great rarity—it's always a collector's item."

"You mean to say it's worth more than sterling?" the woman insists skeptically.

The auctioneer is losing his temper. "Great Day in the morning!" he bursts out again with his favorite exclamation. "Didn't I just explain that every piece of Sheffield plate in the world is a genuine antique? You can walk into Tiffany's any day and buy all the sterling silver you want—but if it's Sheffield plate you're after, you'll have to hunt for it, and it's a big question whether you can find any or not." With a defiant shake of the head he glares at the woman. "But, my friend, you are wasting our valuable time for there are others here who are ready and anxious to bid on this rare and unusual tea set. In fact," he brandishes a telegram in his hand, "I have an advance offer of sixty dollars for the set—do I hear the seventy? Sixty dollars I am offered, do I hear the seventy?"

A hand goes up near the center of the auditorium. "Seventy I have, do I hear the eighty—I'm listening, do I hear the eighty?"

Down in front a hand goes slowly up with five fingers extended.

"Seventy-five I have, now do I hear the eighty?"

He rings the changes on this for some time, determined not to give up too easily, but the audience is equally determined not to pay any more. Finally he leans his chunky body forward, a matted lock of hair dangling over his left ear. "All I'm asking you to do is to nod your head or raise your hand. Do you want me to believe that you'd rather sit there like a bump on a log? You don't want me to think that you're like my old friend Rastus who was known as the laziest man in Corncob County, Kentucky? A stranger stopped at his cabin one morning and knocked on the door. Mandy, wife of Rastus, peered out. 'Wha' foh you-all knockin' on my door?'

" 'I want to see Rastus—is he anywhere around?'

" 'Ah doan rightly know,' said Mandy. 'He done took his ole ax and went to de woods dis mawnin' to cut me some billets fo' de stove. Foh a while Ah heared him choppin',' she stepped outside and shaded her eyes with her hand, 'but Ah doan see nuthin of him now.'

" 'Where was he doin' all this choppin'?'

"Mandy pointed. 'Down yonder by that there big tree next them woods.'

"The stranger squinted up his eyes and looked. 'All I can see is a couple of dark objects layin' on the ground—look like logs to me.'

"Mandy nodded her head. 'Yassuh, one of 'em suah is a log.'

" 'Yeah,' said the stranger, 'but which one?'

"Mandy chuckled and wagged her head wisely. 'You-all stand right where you is, and watch them two dark objects close, and if one of 'em moves—*that* one's the log!' "

The auctioneer laughs as jovially at his own story as if he had never heard it before; and after the room has quieted down he resumes, "and now to get on with our auction. . . ."

Sale by auction is almost as old as the eternal hills. And most certainly it is as old as war—one of man's earliest enterprises— for it is supposed to have originated on the field of battle where victors had captured more spoils than they could conveniently carry away and desired to turn their loot into money or at least into something more easily portable. To start an auction on the battlefield the victorious soldier would thrust his spear into the ground to attract attention, pile his loot around it and call for bids.

This proved to be such a successful method of selling that it was copied in the marts of trade. People would put their salable goods on display and send the town crier around ringing his bell and shouting "Auction! Auction!" to attract a crowd. The auction has been referred to by Juvenal, Cicero, and other classical writers, though the earliest recorded mention was by Herodotus, the so-called Father of History, who wrote in his *Chronicles* of the sale of beautiful maidens to the highest bidder in the luxury-loving city of Babylon which he visited in the fifth century B.C.

"Every year," he says in Book I, "these things were done in each village. They gathered together all the maidens that were come to the season of marriage; and round them stood a multitude of men; and an auctioneer caused them to stand up one by one and sold them. He sold the comeliest of all first; then when she had been sold for much money, he would sell the next after her in comeliness. And they were sold for matrimony."

It might as well have been for slavery, for the maidens had no choice in the matter. They were knocked down to the highest bidder and no questions asked except if he had the money to cover his bid and could furnish a satisfactory surety that he would marry the girl. Nor was there any way that the parents of the maiden could prevent or influence the sale. The rights of the bidder came first. No father was allowed to give a daughter in marriage even if he had a most desirable candidate pleading for her hand. She must be sold to the highest bidder since the state had a stake in the proceeds as in the case of the present-day income tax.

Love and affection had no more part in the transaction than as if the buyer had been purchasing a horse. The maiden was merely a beautiful animal. Other connoisseurs had looked her over and had liked her lines, for they had done some stubborn bidding before they would let her go. Like a horse, she might turn out to be gentle and break to harness easily; or on the contrary she might be too high-spirited and develop into a kicker or an outlaw, or she might be a cribber. But unlike a horse, you couldn't try her before you would buy her—you had to take her on a gamble. However, if she proved not to be a virgin the buyer could return her and get his money back.

Usually the buyer went directly to the priest for he could not get full possession of his bargain until after the marriage. It was a rather exciting way to enter into the state of matrimony: no bridesmaids, no showers, no ushers with their horseplay, their tin cans, and old shoes; just a few "I do's" and "I will's" and you'd be off on your honeymoon with a perfect stranger. An interesting variation on an old theme.

While these marriage customs seem preposterously unfair to families with desirable daughters, they could prove to be a boon to the parents of a maiden who was ugly, misshapen, repulsive-looking, or otherwise so undesirable that nobody was willing to make a bid for her. However, the marriage laws provided an escalator clause by allowing the auctioneer to pay a dot or bonus to customers who were crude enough to care nothing about the good looks of a wife. The funds for this dowry were taken from the extravagant prices collected on the sales of the most beautiful and desirable maidens.

"And when," says Herodotus, "the auctioneer had gone through the comeliest, selling them, he called up the worst-favored, one at a time, even to the halt, and asked who would take the least for marrying her."

The bidding now became the exact opposite to that of the regular auction. Instead of starting low and going up, it started high and went down.

"Who'll take her for 1000 sesterces?" the auctioneer would cry, pointing to a cross-eyed woman with a club-foot. "She's a bargain at that figure. She's well-built and strong, she can be useful, and they all look alike in the dark of the night. Who wants her for that price?"

Several hands go up. It was a liberal price.

"One thousand I have, several times over. Who'll make it nine hundred? Do I hear the nine?"

A squint-eyed old man in the rear raises a hand.

"Nine hundred I have," chants the auctioneer. "Do I hear the eight?"

And so it would go until the halt, the lame, and the ill-favored were married off with a dot that might amount to fifty or one hundred dollars of our present-day money.

Though this auction of the maidens was no doubt thrilling and exciting to the historian as well as to the prospective bidders, it must have been to no small extent terrifying to a family with a marriageable daughter, especially if she happened to be beautiful. The daughter may have had her dreams and hopes, but she must also have had her nightmares about the stranger who would lead her away from the auction block and thrust her into a totally unknown household as his wife.

And the sorrowing parents must have been greatly perturbed over the uncertain fate of their daughter who might be bid in by a foreigner and carried off to a strange and unknown country with unusual or outlandish laws where they might never see her again. Or she might be bought by a man with a collector's instinct and a plurality of wives and numerous offspring.

While this auction of the maidens was notable for its barbarity, there occurred in Rome at a somewhat later date an auction which many historians have regarded as one of the most preposterous sales of all time, for it placed on the auction block the entire Roman Empire which was then sprawled out all the way from Syria on the east to the Danube on the north, and to Britain on the west.

It happened in the first century A.D. when Pertinax, an aging senator, had just ascended the throne upon the murder of his predecessor through a plot contrived by the praetorians. This once-noble body of warriors created as a personal guard for the Emperor had deteriorated into a gang of cutthroat politicians who, finding Pertinax too honorable for them, boldly contrived his murder.

But after the killing the praetorians discovered that they had gone too far, for they could find nobody foolhardy enough to take over the throne. Having cast about in vain for a successor they decided to sell out and make a cleanup, and thereupon issued a presumptuous proclamation from the ramparts to the effect that at a certain time and place the entire Roman Empire would be offered for sale under the hammer to the highest bidder.

All within hearing were stunned. Naturally they looked to the senate for action, but to their astonishment the senators remained silent. Being old and frightened, they huddled together waiting for somebody else to do something. At last Senator Didius Julianus, probably the wealthiest and certainly one of the most courageous of all the senators, rose angrily to his feet and spoke with great eloquence, urging his fellow members to stand up and organize for the salvation of their country. But not a man stood up, not a fist was clenched.

Angry, distraught, and thoroughly aroused, Didius strode from the Forum, and at the time appointed for the sale he appeared at the camp of the praetorians where the auction was to be held. There to his astonishment, in addition to great crowds of the terrified populace, he found Sulpicianus, the father-in-law of the murdered Pertinax, who had come "to make his own bargain with the soldiers," as Anthon the historian says, "not knowing that Pertinax had already been murdered." And so the auction began.

Sulpicianus, a man of modest means, started with a moderate bid; but Didius, with all his wealth behind him, would not deign to bid in less than thousands. Sulpicianus came tagging along with moderate bids as far as his resources lasted. But he was a cautious fellow and, after all, only a father-in-law; and when he had reached his limit he dropped out and the Empire was knocked down to Didius.

Having been hailed as the winner and proclaimed Emperor by popular vote, Didius returned to the city at the head of a vast procession led by the cheering praetorians. The senators with their usual servility drew a long breath of relief and cheerfully accepted Didius as Emperor.

If, however, either the senators or the praetorians regarded the incident as closed they were greatly mistaken; for when word of these disgraceful goings-on reached the far-flung Roman armies at their foreign stations, the generals broke camp and started posthaste for Rome, each army nominating its commander for the office of Emperor. Septimus Severus, in command of Upper Panonia, where he was in charge of the crack Danube command, with the best army, the shortest distance to go, and the best route to travel, was the first to arrive.

He came marching into the city with colors flying and

trumpets blasting, and took it over like a conquering hero, making virtual prisoners of the praetorians, the senate, and the entire population. The craven praetorians, with the money of Didius still jingling in their purses, deserted the Emperor they had so recently crowned and climbed tardily on the military bandwagon of the conquering hero. Then to prove their loyalty to him they burst into the Royal Palace and captured the unfortunate Didius who quietly submitted and begged to be allowed to go into exile. But his captors were out for a Roman holiday and they hacked off his head and carried it into the streets where it could be more conveniently insulted and spat upon—and the Empire went on its bloody way to its destined decline and fall.

CHAPTER TWO

THE AUCTIONEER DISCOVERS AMERICA

ACCORDING TO THE ILLUSTRIOUS MR. CHURCHILL, THE ROMANS
had a flair for civilizing the countries they conquered, and when
some fifty-four years before Christ the invading legions of
Caesar's army had put the chariots of Britain to headlong flight,
the real civilization of the English-speaking peoples began.
Somewhere along the way the Romans had incorporated into
their *Corpus Juris Civilis* some sketchy laws on auctioneering
later adopted by the British and still to be found in the English
Common Law.

Whether the Roman invaders brought the auction with them
or found it already a going concern on British soil is neither
here nor there; but the word *auction* was undoubtedly derived
from the Latin *auctio* meaning "increase." As early as the days
of Christopher Columbus, Henry VII promulgated a law to the
effect that no person should conduct a public sale of goods or
property without first obtaining a license from the proper
authorities and paying an annual fee therefor; and all un-
licensed persons were strictly prohibited from selling goods or
merchandise by "public outcry" without a severe penalty for
violation.

Auctioneering must even then have been of some importance or Henry would not have bothered with the machinery for licensing it.

And thus it happened that the auction came to America as part of the Common Law and was more or less taken for granted wherever there were English settlements along the Atlantic coast. With the scarcity of personal property and effects, it is quite probable that for a time auctioneering was regarded as only a part-time occupation among the colonists. There were, however, certain legal situations which required the services of an auctioneer, such as the sale of a delinquent's property for the payment of his debts, or forced sales of any kind.

The Pilgrims had come to the New World primarily for religious freedom, and at great financial cost for which they had gone deeply in debt, an obligation which they had expected to pay primarily by salting cod for the breakfast tables of Britain, and by trading with the Indians for skins of the beaver, mink, or any other kind of precious furs to keep milady warm and make her look lush and beautiful.

Soon after they were established in America, however, their program narrowed down to furs and clapboard, for they found that fishery for the market was vastly different from going fishing for fun. There must be sturdy fishing smacks and good seamanship, and a great quantity of gear was required, as well as a very considerable degree of know-how, to say nothing of a modicum of good luck. The truth is that the company had been living on Cape Cod Bay for months before they succeeded in catching enough fish for a hearty breakfast.

The fishery project having been abandoned, their next effort at getting themselves out of debt was through fur trading. They had by this time established reasonably friendly relations with some of the Indians who were now coming into Plymouth quite freely, bringing with them a basket of corn, a freshly killed deer, or a wild turkey for trading. But no furs had been brought in, and with the coming of the first cold days in the fall a party of Pilgrims sailed their shallop up the coast a few miles to make a call on the Massachusetts tribe where it was reported that quite a number of squaws had been seen wearing beaver coats. On their arrival at the Indian village they found the report to be true. They powwowed for a time and invited the Indians to bring their furs when they were ready to barter, to which the redskins agreed.

When they were ready to leave the visitors were followed to the shallop by some of the Indian women, mostly young maidens, all clad in coats of beaver which the Pilgrims greatly admired. They would have been glad to barter for the coats but courteously forebore. However, after they had reached the shallop and were exhibiting some of their trade goods, the maidens were so tempted by the bright beads and glittering trinkets that they peeled off their coats to make a deal, thereby stripping themselves literally, for they were wearing nothing underneath. They quickly bartered away their coats for a bit of tinsel and a handful of beads, and then began breaking off branches with which to make their nudity less conspicuous.

One can almost see those goggle-eyed Pilgrim Fathers whipping out their knives from the belts of their baggy knickers and leading the maids over into the bushes to cut a seemly twig or two to cover a pretty lady's nakedness. One of the voyagers, doubtless referring to the branches, later confided to his diary that the Indian maidens showed more modesty than some English women he had known; and the Governor noted in his journal that the visit had been made "to trade with the natives; which they performed, and found kind entertainment."

When the time came for leaving the party broke up with the feeling that friendly relations had been firmly established. The Pilgrims promised to come again, and very probably they did, for they were indefatigable traders. But trade goods were not easy to come by, and we are told that on another occasion when

the Governor heard that a trading post on Monhegan Island off
the coast of Maine was going out of business, he and his crew
sailed the shallop more than 150 miles up the stern and rock-
bound coast to attend the auction where he spent some 400
pounds bidding in tools, trinkets, and gewgaws to be traded to
the Indians.

The most useful purchase made on the journey was a quantity
of wampum obtained from the captain of a Dutch trading ship
which happened to come into port while the shallop was still
there. The Indians preferred wampum to real money, which had
no value to them except as a souvenir, and they were as pleased
with a penny as with a pound. But show an Indian a yard or
two of beads and he would trade you the furs right off his
squaw's back.

It has been said that the Bible and the beaver were the main-
stays of the Pilgrims, the Good Book saving their souls, and the
beavers paying their bills. This was no doubt true in the early
days, but it could not go on indefinitely. It did last long enough,
however, to enable the Pilgrims to pay off their very considerable debt to their merchant partners in England, and for some
of them to make themselves fairly well-to-do. But busy as the
beavers are reputed to be, they could not keep up with the
demands of civilization, and like the great whooping crane they
gradually disappeared from the New England scene.

With the passing of the beaver, relations between the Indians
and the white man deteriorated rapidly. The white man who
had hitherto been content to confine his settlements to the
coastal regions now turned to lumbering and agriculture, two
occupations which required land and more land; and since
clearing and cultivating woodland is not conducive to good
hunting and fishing, the savages were slowly driven back. They
never could be made to understand how the white man merely by
discovering land could claim ownership of it, and they withdrew
slowly and sullenly with many a bloody massacre of the whites.

At last King Philip, greatest of all the New England chieftains, was goaded into an all-out war with the combined forces of the New England colonies determined upon his extermination. The Bible commonwealths, steadfastly believing that the Indians were the degenerate descendants of the Lost Tribes of Israel, took a holy joy in slaughtering them; and having trapped the Indians at the mouth of the Mystic River not far from Sherwood Island, they fell upon the savages with religious frenzy and butchered them even after they had surrendered, taking no prisoners except a few squaws and papooses who were "mercifully" sold into slavery.

A lesser conflict known as the Pequot War ended in the same way with the complete obliteration of the tribe. In reading the details of these gory affairs one is inclined to wonder which side was that of the unredeemed savage although Cotton Mather refers to this Indian warfare as a "sweet sacrifice" to the Heavenly Father.

This virtual extinction of the eastern tribes removed the final barrier to the settlement of the entire back country of the New England colonies, and with the power of the Indians broken and all this land open to settlement, shrewed speculators who always seem to appear when something is to be had for little or nothing, were waiting in line to acquire the most acreage for the least money.

Then too, the public, now that the wide-open spaces were safe from the war whoop and the scalping knife, had developed a vast hunger for elbowroom and fresh air. They were bored with living in a tiny overcrowded house or cabin on an acre of land or less, and when the land speculators opened their developments and called in the auctioneers, bidders came flocking in droves with their wallets in their hands.

And now there came a great change in the life of the local auctioneer. There is little mention of him in the early history of the New England states, still he must have been right there for he was needed as an appraiser wherever there were courts of law or forced sales of any kind. A death in a family, or a marriage could possibly bring on an auction and frequently did, though probably not often enough to suit the Yankee auctioneer who liked to hear the sound of his own voice frequently enough to keep the larder well filled; then suddenly the auctioneer found himself the most needed man in the whole of New England. The shortage was acute, but not for a very long period, for almost any good Yankee can sell things, and given a voice he could, with a little practice, become a very satisfactory auctioneer.

A great restlessness had come over all New England. Hardly anybody wanted to stay put. The urge to go somewhere else seemed to be universal. Whole towns that did not like their location for one reason or another would simply pull up stakes and go somewhere else, selling out if they could, and going just the same if they couldn't. Some of them made no effort to sell, but when they saw the others going they fell in behind.

This vast mass movement has been described by historians as "towns on the march." But it was not entirely a movement of towns, for many of the groups were without municipal or civic background. A number of them were religious splinters breaking off from the mother church. Some were family groups with a strong strain of paternalism; they wanted family farms or homes to be on adjoining land. Others were congenial friends wishing to free themselves of undesirable neighbors while opportunities for cheap land were still available. However, a large proportion of the movement was made up of people lured by the deeply-felt desire to own a sizable piece of land—something that they never could have had in the old country. And it is safe to say that all were impelled to some extent by a longing to better their condition.

At long last the auctioneer was to have his taste of glory. He was everywhere in demand. There was hardly enough of him to go around, for not only was he selling the land, but he was also auctioning off the personal property that was being left behind, since not all of one's furniture and other personal effects could be taken on a cross-country jaunt through the wilderness, for there was not at the time an established road in the whole of America. From an indolent fellow waiting around for somebody to die, or move, or run amuck with the law, the auctioneer was as much in demand as a doctor during a time of epidemic. You couldn't just call him in—you had to make an appointment and take your turn.

It was not only the old inhabitants who had to be reckoned with, but the innumerable immigrants from the whole of Europe who were now pouring into the country on any old tub that was seaworthy enough to get clearance papers for the journey, most of them panting to reach the New World before all the cheap land had been taken up, not realizing how much there was of it extending off in the direction of the westering sun.

And so it went, day after day, group after group, town after town. Settlements seemed to spring up out of the ground like mushrooms after a rain. Country that was wilderness one day was crawling the next day with ambitious human beings grubbing to carve a home out of the forest primeval; and the colonial land offices were adding new townships to the records at a bewildering rate, for land was not only plentiful, but was dirt cheap.

Insofar as individual buyers were concerned land auctions were running wide open every day of the week until the early blue laws reminded people to remember the Sabbath day to keep it holy. In the case of groups or societies, a company was formed, an allotment assigned and surveyed by the colonial authorities, and the lots or farms auctioned off to the highest bidders among the members. But because of the absence of wilderness roads hardly any of the land was auctioned off on location. Property for the allotment of Canaan near the north-west corner of Connecticut was auctioned at New London, some eighty miles away as the crow flies, to buyers practically none of whom had ever actually seen an acre of it. Why the sale of this mountain town should have taken place so far away and in a seafaring village is somewhat puzzling. All they had to go by was a map, but the sale was a great success with bids starting at sixty pounds, the highest rate for any part of Litchfield County.

Land for the settlement of Goshen was auctioned off at New Haven, and the land for Litchfield was sold in Hartford and became a trading station for what was then called the North-west Frontier. And as the coastal colonies filled up and became states, their claims of ownership kept reaching farther and farther toward the western horizon, some of the old maps showing Massachusetts as including territory now in the state of Ohio, and Connecticut in the Western Reserve almost to the Illinois River. Just what part the auctioneers may have taken in these grandiose claims does not appear.

One of the curious aspects of the great New England "land rush," however, is the fact that none of the larger towns seemed at all interested in becoming big cities. When a thriving town reached a population of a thousand or two, and the village green seemed overcrowded on market day, a likely spot for a new settlement would be selected and auctioneers employed to sell to newcomers homesites in a new town. Thus Woodbridge, Wallingford, and Hamden were started by New Haven as "daughter towns," to keep newcomers away, and Danbury was settled by eight families from Norwalk presumably for the same reason.

It was the land rush that gave the auctioneers of New England their first real opportunity in the New World; and they made such a resounding success of their sales of the untamed lands running into millions of acres, that they firmly established themselves as an indispensable part of the New England way of life.

Off to the south in the other great English-speaking colony at Jamestown, there were no "towns on the march" to spur the auctioneers into superhuman action. Still they were there, and were performing their usual occupation just as they had done in the homeland. They had gone through the years of disillusionment and despair, harassed as they were by Indian warfare, starvation, disease, and internal squabbles. These colonists had somehow survived where the earlier colonists had failed.

It was not, however, until colonist John Rolfe had married into the family of Chief Powhatan by taking the Indian maid Pocohontas as his bride that livable peace with the redskins was finally achieved. The marriage of Rolfe not only put an end to the sniping and scalping in Virginia, but placed him in a position to learn the Indian secrets of tobacco culture and curing, which with his own knowledge of cross-breeding brought a vast improvement of the Virginia leaf and made possible the great Tobacco Commonwealth of Virginia.

From the beginning of Jamestown the colony was dominated not so much by the crowned heads of Britain as by the uncrowned heads of the English gentry who arrived in numbers with the first flotilla, and kept on arriving with every boatload, especially after the execution of Charles I when a large number of Royalists decided that a sea voyage to Virginia would be good for their health. They arrived just in time for the opening of the tobacco boom on which they capitalized in a big way.

Large tracts of the lovely fertile Virginia countryside were easily acquired by those in the know, and the time was not far off when the tobacco auctioneers were running their sales into the millions, and great mansions surprisingly like the famous English country houses were going up on the magnificent landscape.

By this time the wives and children of the Royalists and the gentry had arrived, and slavery had been installed to overcome the great labor shortage, for large plantations with thousands of acres cannot be profitably worked without adequate labor, and the free working class of Virginia were by this time raising tobacco for themselves on their own small farms. Then, too, the great tobacco aristocracy was on its way and rapidly gathering recruits from across the ocean where times were not as good.

Among the newcomers was John Washington, grandfather of George, who migrated to Virginia on the crest of the tobacco prosperity and built a beautiful country house on a large tract in the smart "Northern Neck" between the Rappahannock and the Potomac rivers and became a highly respected citizen and a successful tobacco planter with a working force of over three hundred slaves. His son Augustus was the father of George, who was born in 1732 and left an orphan at the age of twelve. By the time George was of age he had inherited Mount Vernon and had gone there to live.

In those leisurely days of the stagecoach and the windjammer, true elegance in the arts of decoration and homemaking was not to be had by ordering over the telephone. Choice silverware and glass, handsome fabrics and furniture, indeed, all the objects of art and virtu had to be ordered abroad or purchased at public auction when death or some other agency of change had brought on a dispersal settlement of one of the great estates.

George Washington being a gentleman of most excellent taste, is said to have selected all the furnishings for his own home. Indeed, it was whispered around that he even ordered the gowns and the entire wardrobe of Martha and the rest of his household, placing the orders through his factors in London. In those days an auction sale at one of the great country houses—or plantations as they preferred to call them—was indeed an event which brought opulent buyers from a wide area, and George Washington rarely missed one if it was anywhere within reach. It taxes the imagination, however, to picture the future Father of His

Country wagging a long forefinger at the auctioneer while engaging in a spirited bidding duel with a powdered and scented colonial dame determined to have a certain silver porringer even if that young Mr. Washington should bid it up to far more than its worth.

However, inventories of some of the old auctions would indicate that young Mr. Washington usually got what he set out to buy—but only if the price was right, even though it might be a mere matter of shillings, for he was no spendthrift. There is still in existence a record of an auction at the plantation of Lord Fairfax of Belvoir, a close friend and neighbor who was moving back to England where he already had a magnificently furnished country house.

On the list are entries which show that Washington bid in such scarce items as pickle pots, bolsters, pillows, and bottles (probably decanters), for his own use. He did not stop at these trifles but went on and bid in a very elegant six-legged mahogany tambour sideboard for twelve pounds and five shillings. He made other purchases that day which included some small side tables that, together with the sideboard, may still be seen at Mount Vernon.

It is amusing to think of the future President, the most dignified and beloved of all our presidents, as calling out bids for such items as a toasting fork, a featherbed, some odd pewter plates, and from the Baron's own room, a shaving table for himself. Washington's most elegant purchase of the day was a four-poster bedstead (another place where he must occasionally have slept) with slender posts extending almost to the ceiling, each topped with a brass ball and eagle. There were no over-hanging side curtains, but a scalloped ruffle several inches in depth formed a hollow rectangle around the tops of the posts.

Washington was a good customer that day, for his purchases amounted to some two hundred pounds sterling.

CHAPTER THREE

THE COLOR LINE

THOUGH THE AUCTIONEERS OF THE OLD DOMINION HAD NO reason for suspecting such a thing at the time, they had a stroke of good luck in 1619 when, according to John Rolfe, the English husband of Pocahontas, a Dutch trader dropped anchor at Jamestown and sold the planters twenty "Negars," thereby earning the dubious honor of introducing slavery in the English colonies.

Whether these slaves were auctioned off or were sold at a set price of so much a head does not appear in the brief record put down by Rolfe, but they were the beginning of a development on the American mainland of the greatest slave market of the Western World.

The tobacco boom was then in its infancy, with the European market begging for the Virginia leaf and the planters unable to supply more than a small proportion of the demand because of the shortage of workmen in the Colony. Hitherto Virginia had depended for its labor supply on indentured servants and convicts sent over from the crowded jails of London. But Britain was not turning out jailbirds fast enough to satisfy the demands of the landed proprietors who were now having their first opportunity to consider the use of slave labor. However, being inexperienced in the handling of blacks they were proceeding cautiously.

No doubt the Virginia planters looked the slaves over with a jaundiced eye. The males and females were virtually naked, being clad only in breechclouts. Emaciated as they were from the hardships of the journey the men had big muscles, and the women looked strong and well developed.

Like any beast of burden, the blacks were unbroken and would have to be taught to work. Then, too, there was the language difficulty; not one of them could speak anything but African gibberish. And being untamed, they would have to be kept in shackles until proper pens and shelters could be built. However, after they were once broken in they would be permanent help, good for a lifetime if they could be kept from running away.

Doubtless the Dutchman laughed when they spoke about the possibility of running away. Dogs could easily be trained to run them down; and besides, where could they run to in this God-forsaken land infested with hostile Indians? And when the question of the morality of slavery was mentioned it was quickly disposed of by quotations from the Bible in which slavery was spoken of a number of times—but not discountenanced or forbidden. And no doubt the Dutchman brought up the matter of breeding, for it was one of the big selling points. Just match up a couple, put them in together, and let nature take its course. They were wonderful breeders and would produce about once a year.

Marriage? Absolutely unnecessary, and in most countries illegal.

And so the Jamestown planters bought themselves twenty "Negars," though history fails to record what became of them, who bought them, how much was paid for them, whether they left any descendants, or how long it was before other slaves were landed in Virginia. However, the insatiable demand of the tobacco and cotton culture turned eventually to the slaves and swept the southern states like wildfire, reaching the million mark by the turn of the century, and four million by the opening shot of the Civil War.

Blind to the moral issues at stake, which were being magnificently beclouded by the eminent oratory of the great statesmen of the South, the auctioneers in their quest of the almighty dollar, threw themselves into the slave traffic with such abandon that their calling became as unsavory as that of overseer or slave driver. They made the money—but at the cost of their good name.

There was hardly a hamlet south of the Mason and Dixon Line without its slave market where the hopeless unfortunates could be bought and sold as freely as steers in the cattle country, or horses in Kentucky. And one might as well expect friendly commiseration from a hangman as any feeling of pity or compassion from a slave auctioneer, for his sole interest was to sell the slaves for all he could get—and pocket a fat commission.

Whether the victims were sold down the river or up the river made little difference to him. He had no qualms about parting a husband and wife, or a parent and child. To him a slave was a mere commodity, an "article"—to use the jargon of the auction block—and he knocked it down to the highest bidder with no more compunction than as if he were selling a pig.

Albert Bushnell Hart tells in his very excellent book, *Slavery and Abolition* of a woman who saw a female slave put on the auction block quite obviously ill. She had a bad cough and complained of a severe pain in her side, at which the auctioneer blurted out to bystanders:

"Don't pay no mind to what she says, gentlemen. I've already told you that she's a shammer. Her health is good enough. Damn her humbug! Give her a touch or two of the cowhide and I'll warrant you she'll do your work. Speak, gentlemen, before I knock her down—now what am I offered?"

Pregnancy was no excuse for not putting a woman up for sale. Indeed, the auctioneer was glad to have them come that way, for they were ordinarily treated as two, the auctioneer making the occasion hilarious with salacious jokes to amuse the crowd which was always ready for a wisecrack at the expense of the victim on the block.

Very few of the slave auctioneers regarded the black as belonging to the human family. He was considered as just another "critter." On the auction bills slaves were almost invariably listed among the farm animals. Sometimes they would be included among the horses and cows; again they would be listed with the chickens and pigs; and on one occasion two Negroes were grouped with "one jennet, a pair of cart wheels, a side-saddle, and a new-milch cow with a calf by her side."

It was an ordinary sight at an auction to see a swaggering bully take unwarranted liberties with the pretty, light-complexion mulattos. They would caress a girl's bosom, follow the contour of her body with their coarse hands, and even lift her skirts for a look underneath while the auctioneer would stand leering approvingly and not missing anything.

A painful sight at an auction was to see a pleasant and agreeable-looking slave girl bought and dragged away by a coarse and loud-mouthed ruffian muttering brazenly about what he was going to do to her when he got her home. Not infrequently a pretty, light-skinned young octoroon would be bought as a birthday gift for a friend or a member of the family, or even to pay a gambling debt—possibly a wager lost on a horse race. And there were cases where a favorite preacher would be bought by his own congregation and freed so that he could not be sold down the river or taken away by a purchaser from some far-distant point.

Before emancipation put an end to the practice, long chain gangs or "coffles" were frequently to be seen shuffling along the country roads. They might be going only from one plantation to another, or even from one state to another, though the longer journeys were usually made by steamboat. There might be only ten or twenty shackled together, or there could be as many as one hundred; and Mortimer Thompson writes of one famous case in which there were nearly five hundred in a single coffle where a large plantation owner who had gambled away a fortune was selling off his slave holdings to pay his debts. Since on his several plantations there was no suitable dispersion point for so extensive an auction, he was moving the slaves to a large warehouse located on the site of a former race track near one of the large cities of the Deep South.

The slaves were chained in long files of twenty or thirty, the women segregated from the men, with each individual carrying in a box or bag all his or her worldly possessions; for after living with the one owner nobody knows how long, the entire company was to be sold under the hammer—and scattered to all points of the compass, probably never to see one another again.

They reached their destination on Sunday afternoon when the company came shuffling in, dusty and disheveled, the women carrying their packs on their heads, and many of them with babies in their arms or slung on their backs, and the men with their boxes and blanket rolls on their shoulders or strapped where they could be most conveniently carried. The women in their bright calicoes and many-colored kerchiefs looked like so many gypsies; but the men in their coarse clothing resembled exactly what they were—a gang of tired field hands, most of them barefooted and some who had started out in boots were now carrying them in their hands or hung over their shoulders.

At frequent intervals at the sides of the files were white slave drivers or overseers armed with sturdy ox-gads with which they would from time to time whack the slaves on the ankles or the back with a threat or a curse to keep them from lagging. Crowds from the dusty roadside watched the caravan as it went shuffling past, calling or whistling at the girls, and hurling coarse com-

ments at the men, some of whom kicked up their heels or made
other clownish gestures or grimaces calculated to get a laugh.

The warehouse, which had been converted from an immense
barn, had been subdivided with men's quarters at one end of
the building, a room for the women at the other end and, in
between, a large amphitheater along which four stagings had
been erected for the auctioneers. Former horse stables in the
rear had been converted into toilet accommodations that even
the horses must have snorted at. In a barracoon at one end was
a trough of scummy water in which any necessary washing
could be done.

Once they were inside the iron gates the tired travelers col-
lapsed to the ground or sat on their packs and bundles as they
awaited the removal of their shackles. Upon being freed of the
shackles they were admitted to the building, being checked at
the door to be sure that none was missing. Inside the building
they were herded to their quarters, where they were constantly
under guard.

The only provision for the comfort of the slaves was a little
fresh straw sprinkled on the floor where they were supposed
to sleep. Presently food was brought in for them and served with
about as much style as if they had been a herd of swine. After
they had finished eating they threw themselves down on the
floor, pillowed their heads on their bundles, and were locked
in for the night with armed guards posted at the doors.

They were fed again the next morning soon after daybreak,
and were told to wash and clean themselves up so they would
be sure to bring a high price and get a good home. By ten o'clock
the slaves had been divided into four groups, one for each auctioneer, and were waiting on the staging for the selling to begin
while the auctioneer moved around among them tidying them
up and instructing them how to behave. He gives a hitch to the
sleeve of one and orders another to tuck in his shirttail. He tells
one of the girls to brush her hair back out of her eyes, and

indicates to another who has been nursing a baby that she should close the front of her dress.

At a given signal all the auctioneers go into action, each one bringing to the front of the staging his first offering of the day.

"You—Julia! Come out here!"

As a pretty light-skinned octoroon stepped nervously forward, a tall countryman in a broad-brimmed hat pushed his way forward through the crowd. Obviously an outdoor man, he was wearing both a knife and a pistol in his belt indicating that he had come there to buy and had money on his person. As he reached the staging he stopped with a booted foot on the bottom step and raised his hand authoritatively to halt the auctioneer who had already begun his opening remarks.

"Never mind all that," the countryman interrupted. "Just hold it until I have a chance to look this article over."

The auctioneer paused and glared at him. "You mean you want to examine her?" he demanded.

"That's what I said!"

"Well—go ahead and examine all you want to, Mister. We ain't got nothing to hide. This gal has never been away from her ma. She's a prime house servant and a good cook."

"Aw, cut the palaver," the countryman said as he went tramping up the steps to the platform.

The girl drew back and glanced quickly at her mother for instructions. With all the noise and confusion being made by the other three auctioneers it was impossible to tell whether the girl spoke or not, but it could be seen that her mother had nodded to her before the visitor had gripped her arm.

He leaned over until his face was close to her body, and sniffed her up and down. Then he drew back and stared closely into her face. "Open your mouth," he commanded gruffly.

She agreeably but shyly complied, throwing back her head and displaying a perfect set of snow-white teeth. He peered inside, back and forth, then sniffed at her breath. "Not bad," he said. Then scrutinizing her bosom he asked, "Any padding in there?"

The girl struggled to wrench herself loose but he was too strong for her. "No, suh," she cried. "There shuah ain't!"

By this time the crowd was shouting with laughter. He held her a moment longer, then suddenly whirled her around and gave her a smart slap on the behind. "How about here?" he asked as he released his hold and started laughingly down the steps.

The auctioneer stood grinning at this horseplay and after the countryman had disappeared into the crowd he returned to his job of selling slaves. The first bid on the girl was $150 which was quickly raised to $200. It went on at $50 a bid until it reached $750. The countryman took no part in the bidding, and the girl was struck down at $800 and was led away sobbing.

A large number of field hands were next sold along with a kitchen maid or two. Then came a blacksmith who went for $1,000 and a horse trainer who brought $800. After that one of the auctioneers announced that he was about to offer a prime slave family as a unit, and he called them out to the front of the staging. There was George, the father, a fine physical specimen and a prime cotton planter and picker, twenty-seven years old. Next came Sue, his common-law wife, a strapping woman of twenty-six and a prime rice planter. There were two boys, Frank, a lad of six, and Harry who was only two. Some of the bidders were disgruntled because they were not to be sold individually, but the auctioneer had received his instructions and after some discussion they went as a family for $2,400.

Twenty babies were sold that day, some of them being taken from the arms of the weeping mothers, for it was well known that the offspring of a slave mother belonged not to her but to her owner. And there was great interest among the buyers of those babies when a buxom woman on the block when asked to give her occupation replied that she was a wet nurse.

Toward the end of the second day the lame, the halt, and the crippled came up for sale and were bought up by bargain-hunters at one or two hundred dollars, though a man with a clubfoot went for seventy-five, and a ruptured man for only fifty. The highest bid of the sale, a fair-skinned young woman only fractionally Negro, with four nearly white children—and one coal-black throwback—brought over $6,000.

Some five hundred slaves changed owners in the sale and the total take for the auction was slightly less than $400,000. If the remuneration of the auctioneer in those old days was anywhere near what it averages today, which is 15 per cent and upwards, the four auctioneers must have divided a fee of some $60,000 which would have come to $15,000 apiece—a tidy sum for a not too difficult job, and no income tax to think about.

For some unaccountable reason the slave-holding population of the South, though tremendously in the minority, was vastly powerful in proportion to their number; for statistics show that in 1860, out of a population of more than twelve million white persons in the slave states, only a third of a million, or one in thirty-three, was a slaveholder, and of the slaveholders some seventy-seven thousand owned only a single slave, usually a house servant or a general utility worker.

The owner of the slaves in the big race-track sale we have been considering was meticulous about making a farewell gift to each slave sold, all gifts being in money—a silver dollar apiece. That is, a silver dollar to all who had been born; but for the unborn child of a pregnant mother a silver half-dollar was given.

While Virginia is said to have had the largest slave population of any state, New Orleans is claimed to have maintained the greatest number of slave markets of any city in continental America. The docks and waterfront district of the city were lined with barracoons where slaves were chained in groups awaiting buyers, and throughout the city auction blocks were almost as numerous as popcorn stands at Coney Island.

High-toned slave markets were to be found in the more prominent parts of the city, and a very elegant auction block was maintained in the splendid Hotel Royal where well-trained house servants could be rented by single gentlemen as mistresses or sold to the houses in the red-light districts of the city.

With the war a thing of the past the slave auctioneers, being out of a job, drifted off to the cotton and tobacco fields where some of them in all probability developed into tobacco auction-eers. Others joined the migration to Texas and other parts of the country where land was being given away, and where no embarrassing questions were asked about the past history of new arrivals.

CHAPTER FOUR

THE AUCTIONEERS GO TO TOWN

THE SOCIAL STATUS ASSUMED OR ATTAINED BY THE AUCTIONEER in America has varied widely according to the locality in which he lives and operates. In the Bible colonies, such as New England, they were likely to be educated folk who had come to make a new life in a new land where one could walk with God and at the same time breathe the air of freedom. In the non-Bible colonies, such as Jamestown, the ideals were not so high. The newcomers were managed by a board of directors in London much more interested in dividends than in saving souls. They were after the wealth of the world, many of them resolved that once they had acquired a goodly portion of it they would return to the land of their birth to enjoy it.

Mostly it was the underlings who had come to stay, to make a home, to own land—lots of land, which they could never have done in Europe. In between these two extremes were the Dutch who had come to the Island of Manhattan as squatters in 1613, well aware of the broad claims of England to the entire Atlantic coast, based on the discoveries of John Cabot, but were extremely doubtful of her ability to establish ownership of land which she had neither occupied nor paid for.

New Amsterdam had grown to a population of about two hundred before Peter Minuit was sent over as Director General in 1626 with instructions to buy the land from the Indians, which he did at the rate of about seventy-five cents per square mile. Upon obtaining this dubious grant he hurriedly built a fort near the tip of the island to repel invaders and erected a gallows as a sign that he meant business.

A succession of directors general followed Minuit, some good and some not so good, but the colony grew rapidly, and when in 1674 it was surrendered to the English without bloodshed, the rights of the Dutch residents who now numbered some ten thousand were carefully maintained, and New Amsterdam became New York.

Living for centuries across the English Channel from each other the Dutch and the English had much in common. They worshipped the same God, read the same philosophers, revered the same arts and cultures, and inherited many of the same laws and customs. A number of their trade practices were similar, and their rules and regulations for conducting an auction at this time were almost identical. Only a generation was required to iron out their linguistic difficulties in New York, and curiously enough in the social life of Manhattan it was the Dutch who looked down their noses at the English instead of the other way around.

To this day those Dutch names are a mouthful: Peter Bejlvelt, Geurdt Van Gelder, Claes Cornelissen Switz, Dingman Versteeg, Wolfert Gerritsz, Wortendyke Van Kouwenhoven, and there were Van Twillers, Van Hoorns, Vanderbilts, a Roosenvelt or two, a Bronck Bronx, and for a finishing touch, de Neve Sinx.

Among the Dutch and the English as well, the auctioneer had always been classified as a petty officer, on a par, let us say, with a constable or bailiff. Of course he had no power of arrest, but before the podium of the auction block his word was final. It was in his power to stop the bidding whenever his judgment told him that the fair value of the property had been reached or even exceeded. The old-time auctioneers will tell you that the fair value of an article is the highest bid made in an open market. There is a fallacy here, however, so long as the auctioneer is covering a flaw with his thumb or holding the article so that the imperfection is invisible to the bidder. In 1704, according to an item in the Stokes *Iconography*, auctions were held frequently in New York and "make their earnings very well by them, for they treat with good liquor liberally, and generally the bidders pay for it by paying for that which they bid up briskly."

A few years later Stokes tells us that auction sales of books have begun in Boston with the sale of the library of one Ebeneezer Pemberton. But it was not until 1731 that a book auction was held in New York, this important event taking place at the Exchange Coffee House on the corner of Broad and Water Streets. "Numerous public vendues," the report concludes, "were held there in succeeding years."

As time marches on the auctioneer continues in the old familiar way. A mortgage is foreclosed and he sells the property from the Courthouse steps. A crockery store goes into bankruptcy or loses its lease, and there is a gigantic sale of crocks, churns, jugs, and demijohns, along with complete sets of bedroom china. Somebody dies, a family is broken up, and all the household effects come under the hammer. These are common occurrences. They are happening here, there, and everywhere, and are part of the fabric of everyday living.

In May, 1773, the auctioneers of New York were puzzled by an ordinance forbidding the holding of auction sales at night. A few months later the Sons of Liberty kicked over the traces and were holding their famous Boston Tea Party. And not long afterward notices were posted in New York that "draft and saddle horses belonging to the King's services will be sold at auction every Wednesday at the Waggon-yard in Brooklyn, and every Saturday at the Waggon-yard near Fort Knyphausen." What's going on? Is his Majesty selling out or something?

Next it was the British storekeepers who were selling out and quitting the country; and on the Eighteenth of April in 'Seventy-five came the famous ride of Paul Revere, followed by the shot heard round the world—and the fat was in the fire—the War of the American Revolution had begun.

For six agonizing years it dragged along with both armies taking a vacation during the winter months and slaughtering each other throughout the summer. Then at long last Cornwallis surrendered in the fall of 1781, though the Treaty of Paris was not formally signed until September 3, 1783; and even then the last redcoat was not out of the country until almost Christmas.

Up to the time of the Revolution Britain had managed to keep America on a strictly agricultural level by providing us a market for our produce while she furnished us with all the manufactured goods our country could possibly require. It was not a bad arrangement for an undeveloped country, but it did not work out so very well after the war came and Britain blockaded our ports to keep our exportables in and the foreign goods out— and that was when we found it necessary to begin making things for ourselves.

Without machines everything had to be handmade and soon secondhand articles of every kind were at a premium. During the months to come the auctioneers combed the attics of America again and again, searching for things that could be mended or made to do. They also worked in close co-operation with smugglers and blockade runners both on the Atlantic shore and across the Great Lakes from Canada. It is quite possible that most of their sales at that time were made from under the counter.

Somehow they managed to exist and stay in business, and when the war ended some two dozen of them were clustered together in a group of small houses on Water Street in downtown New York opposite the old Coffee House, a locality known as "Auctioneers' Row."

Such a collection of battered pans and kettles, broken chairs and tables, as well as three-legged beds had probably never before been assembled in America. It is safe to say that there was not a whole mirror in the Row, not an uncracked plate, hardly a cup that matched a saucer, and certainly no two alike.

With the coming of peace Britain hastened to renew her mothering attitude by flooding the country with her accumulation of manufactured goods, though keeping a strict embargo on machinery to prevent us from manufacturing things for ourselves. It was not a very friendly peace and lasted only a few decades before Britain began a vicious campaign for the impressment of our seamen for the quite obvious purpose of crippling the development of our fast-growing merchant marine lest we should become a serious competitor in the markets of the world.

Provoking us into another war should have been the last thing for Britain to do if she desired to build up a large trade with us; but she went a step too far, and we, being a cocky young country still strutting a bit from having humbled her in the first war —though not without some very valuable help from her European enemies—brashly declared war. This was in 1812.

When Britain recovered from her fit of temper she sued for peace as soon as she could make such a move without too much loss of face. This second war for independence ended the day before Christmas, 1814, though the final battle at New Orleans was fought two weeks after the treaty of peace was concluded, so sluggish was the means of transportation and communication at the time.

Before the coming of the sewing machine there was no such thing as a ready-made. The gentleman had his clothes turned out by a tailor, and the lady bought her material by the yard and had a dressmaker in for weeks at a time for fifty or sixty cents a day and food. Those were the days when the dry goods stores sold dry goods and little else. Their shelves were piled high with bolts of yard goods containing miles of silks, satins, and all kinds of modish fabrics and textiles. Along with the dry goods there were, of course, needles and pins, thread and buttons, scissors, thimbles. Yarn perhaps, and stockings. But lingerie? Even the word was unknown. And a store in which the yard goods shelves were empty might as well have closed its doors, and a number of smaller stores had done just that for the duration. However, they quickly opened up and dusted off the bare shelves when rumors began to go around that just beyond the horizon was a fleet of merchantmen waiting to land as soon as the treaty had been signed.

At long last on February 11, 1815, out of the morning mists came the good ship *Favorite* under a flag of truce with American and British messengers bringing the treaty of peace which had been signed, sealed, and delivered at Ghent, and put in at the port of New York on the way to Washington.

It was a time of great jubilation. The days of wartime stringency were over. All the barricades came down, the blockade was hastily lifted, and soon a great fleet of British merchantmen heavily laden with goods which had been accumulating in British mills and factories or stored in the warehouses of Canada or Bermuda throughout the war, came majestically up the bay with pennons flying and announced that they were ready for business. And although America didn't stop to realize what was happening, it was the same old dumping program all over again.

They brought not only dry goods, fabrics, and textiles, but all kinds of manufactured goods from needles and pins to anvils, plows, and heavy agricultural implements, and though no attention was called to the matter there was no machinery since that was still on the contraband list.

These were dark days indeed for the auctioneers, for who

would take any interest in bidding on their cracked and damaged castoffs with the market loaded to capacity with bright new merchandise, and more coming in every day?

Since it was a famine market, the prices were high, but customers had gone without for such a long time that during the first year after the war they paid the high prices without a murmur, and in these flush and optimistic times credit was so easy and business so good that the pleased and happy merchants kept buying and overbuying even after they should have seen that the big demand was satiated; and so they were caught in a falling market with heavily extended inventories and a shortage of free-spending customers. And still the harbor was filled with merchantmen clamoring for business.

Suddenly faced by a glut in the market the sea captains realized that they could not return their stocks to England without a terrific loss and probable bankruptcy, and there being no other available market, they turned to the auction rooms as a last resort. Here they ran into the impost duties which the U.S. Customs required to be paid in advance before a foreign cargo could be removed from the ship. Unable to make a bank loan without American signers, they formed a partnership with the auctioneers who were able to engineer enough of a loan to bring the cargo ashore where it was quickly sold under the hammer, and the loot divided, whereupon another cargo would be brought ashore and the operation repeated.

The Americans who had long been starved for low-priced merchandise crowded the auction rooms daily. The news was not long in getting around, and soon customers as well as dealers came flocking in from the surrounding towns. And having developed such an active market, the merchantmen after unloading the cargo sailed out of the harbor and went to Canada or Bermuda, whichever was convenient, and came back with another load. The legitimate American merchandisers had all along been expecting that when once the harbor had been

cleared of the dumping ships the cut-rate auction sales would come to an end, business would return to its former channels, and they would once more have their stores crowded with customers. They were hopeful of business as usual.

But when the merchants discovered that the ships had begun to come back again, they stopped pacing their empty aisles and got down to the serious matter of forming a protective association and starting a drive to put an end to the dumping before the situation became any worse than it already was.

The new association began by attacking the auctioneers, harshly charging them with disloyalty in helping the merchantmen to flood our country with British goods, and they also criticized the public for disloyalty in patronizing the auctions and spending their money for foreign merchandise. However, the public continued to patronize the auctions, very much as a later generation patronized the bootleggers in spite of all the prohibition criticism.

These auction sales may have started honestly enough, but like all cutthroat operations they soon developed bootleg tendencies. After the first few cargoes had been disposed of, the store-owning merchants began to protest that all kinds of imitation goods were being sold as genuine, that packages were being mislabled as to quality and quantity, that all sales were being made on a *caveat emptor* basis without guarantees made or implied, with all the other shabby tricks of the cheat and the charlatan.

They tried unsuccessfully to have the auctioneers prosecuted for fraud and misrepresentation. But the auctioneers, being in the money, laughed off the charges and insisted that they were acting solely as salesmen, and gave notice that anyone having any grievances was requested to take matters up with the London office. And they went on with their auctions, pocketing their ill-gotten gains and growing rich while the legitimate merchants were facing ruin, and the owners of the infant industries were locking their doors and going out to hunt for jobs.

But finally the association, guided by what seemed to be wiser counsels, called a huge mass meeting of their members from all the eastern states at which a memorial containing some five thousand signatures was adopted and sent to Congress asking for relief from the evils of the dumping campaign by the passage of a high enough tariff wall to protect the home industry from the insidious depredations of foreign importation; and further to enact suitable legislation outlawing and forbidding, under penalty of the law, the sale by auction of any and all goods and merchandise imported into the United States from a foreign land.

But they found the Congress a hard nut to crack, for by this time it was well understood in Washington and elsewhere that the Treaty of Paris had resolved none of the controversies over which the recent war had been fought; and both houses of Congress were so fearful of starting another war with Britain that the lawmakers hardly dared to speak above a whisper. While the Congress could not entirely disregard the impressive memorial, neither could they see their way clear to grant the very considerable and possibly hazardous relief demanded by the merchants and manufacturers. So the lawmakers treated the application with polite but effective dilatory tactics while they talked the proposed legislation to death, with only a token raise in the tariff.

As time went on some of the merchants liquidated while they had something left to liquidate. Others sank dejectedly into bankruptcy, while a few of the die-hards degenerated into anonymous pamphleteers, a position from which they derived the satisfaction of having their say about the auctioneers without danger of libel suits or horsewhipping. One of the pamphlets is still to be found in the Yale University Library. It is entitled "Remarks About the Auction System as Practiced in New

York." The author hides behind the nom de plume of "A Plain and Practical Man."

Nobody seems to know exactly when the substantial betterment set in, or where it started; but gradually the European markets came to life and Britain found buyers nearer home to whom she could ship her products. American industry came slowly to its feet and finally began to prosper. Gradually the importing auction marts fell into disuse and the proprietors retired as they could well afford to do, or opened elegant shops on Broadway near Union Square where they could appeal to the carriage trade.

Gradually the surviving merchants pulled themselves out from under, moved from their disheveled places of business a few blocks uptown where they opened new quarters while prosperity came timidly round the corner—and life in America went on into the next phase.

CHAPTER FIVE

AUCTIONEERING GETS A BOOST

SPEAKING LOOSELY AND PROBABLY OUT OF TURN, IT IS MY OPINION that the harmless mania for collecting antiques has done more to elevate the occupation of auctioneering than any other development of the past hundred years. We have already pointed out that in the early days of America the auctioneer was merely a humble citizen with a big voice. He was probably of no more importance to the community than the town crier or the colonial fence viewer who punished children for swinging on other people's gates.

When he was auctioning off a bale of furs bartered from the Indians, or selling the miserable belongings of a pauper who couldn't pay his debts, nobody in the gaping crowd so much as dreamed that his counterpart would one day sit in an easy chair on the rostrum of a modern gallery in New York or any other large city, and auction off in a soft voice two antique Ispahan rugs for $153,000; or on the 23rd of January in the year 1957 would sell at auction for a private owner a collection of antique jewels and other works of art amounting to $2,438,980, thereby breaking all existing American records for a single sale.

We are told on good authority that the first serious collector of American antiques was a New England doctor named Irving W. Lyon. He lived in Hartford, which was noted at the time as a woodworking center and had become locally famous for its carved oaken furniture, especially chests. He began his collecting in 1877 in and around Hartford.

There had been a notable collection of historical relics at the Centennial Exhibition in Philadelphia the preceding year which had aroused unusual interest in things of the past and is generally regarded as the starting point of popular antique collecting in this country, though the word "antique" was not used at the time since America had not been settled long enough to think of itself as antique.

Prior to the Centennial Celebration a household article without historical significance had very little chance of being collected. Age alone was not enough. A chair might be kept as long as it was serviceable, but after it became decrepit or old-fashioned it was usually shoved into the attic or thrown on the woodpile, and unless a distinguished personage like a great jurist or a gallant general had sat in it during some national emergency, there was very little chance of its becoming historical enough to be regarded as a relic.

Being a leading manufacturing area at the time, New England was represented by thousands of exhibits at the Centennial, in addition to which there was an attractive cottage which served as a headquarters for people from the Nutmeg State. It was a roomy building constructed on the lines of the previous century and decorated largely with furnishings from the home of General Israel Putnam, one of the most beloved of New England's native sons. There was probably no finer collection of historical relics in New England at that particular time. In the dooryard of the cottage was a simulated well with an old oaken bucket, moss-covered and ironbound, which hung in the well though it never went down, for there was no water, not even a hole in the ground. However, there was a very elegant water-cooler inside the cottage.

Just inside the door was a spinning wheel, and near the cav-

ernous fireplace was a table made of wood from the famous
Charter Oak which had recently succumbed to a wintry gale,
presumably a hurricane, though never mentioned as such until
the present century. The Charter Oak was greatly loved by
people of the Nutmeg State, who regarded it as a symbol of their
freedom and independence, and when it fell some of the more
sentimental citizens draped the stump with mourning and almost
buried it under wreaths and garlands of flowers. They even
conducted a funeral service with the tolling of bells, the rolling
of muffled drums, the rendition of the "Dead March" from *Saul*
by a military band and eulogies both vocal and printed in the
newspapers all over the country.

Wood from the giant oak was cut up into mementos which
were sold to raise money for a suitable memorial. Later on the
crafty Yankees began kidding themselves, before somebody
else could get there first, by turning out a huge wooden ham
from the lumber of the tree. This was hung in the reception
room at the Exhibition, and nearby was a bin full of wooden
nutmegs, also made from wood of the Charter Oak, which
could be had as souvenirs for fifty cents apiece. And as the
story goes, the cottage receptionist always kept a few real
nutmegs among the imitations to prove that a nutmeg by any
other name could smell as sweet.

Many reminders of "Old Put" were to be found in all parts of
the cottage. There was a fine oil portrait of the General above
the mantel, and perched upon hooks in the old-time fashion was
the long-barreled musket with which he is said to have slain
the wolf in the fabulous den at Pomfret. His brace of pistols and
a powder horn dangled from a peg in the wall. There were old-
style candlesticks perched around in various places, and numerous reminders of the days gone by. To some visitors these were
no more than treasured souvenirs of Old Put; but others must
have been poignantly reminded of things in their own attics.

It probably wasn't any one thing—it must have been a number

of things together—nostalgia, old forgotten recollections coming back, love of possession—nobody seems to know what the impelling urge could have been, but soon after people went home from the exhibition old things began coming out of the attic, the storeroom, the dark closet under the stairs, and given an honorable position in the household. It was at about this time that the secondhand man began to think about becoming an antique dealer, and the antique dealer—if he was smart—took up auctioneering.

The Centennial Exhibition was opened on the 11th of May, 1876, at Fairmont Park in Philadelphia by General Grant, who was nearing the end of his second term at the White House. As his carriage entered the grounds he was greeted with the national anthems of America, Austria, Brazil, France, and Germany rendered by an orchestra under the direction of Theodore Thomas. As the President was taking his seat in the grandstand there came thundering from the orchestra the strains of the "Grand Inauguration March" written for the occasion by Wilhelm Richard Wagner, then at the apex of his career as a composer. Next came a prayer followed by a chorus of a thousand voices singing the "Centennial Hymn" written by John Greenleaf Whittier, and ending with a cantata by Sidney Lanier and Dudley Buck.

The local talent having been heard from, the President of the United States declared the Exhibition officially opened. A salute of one hundred guns followed, during which a procession of official visitors formed and marched to Machinery Hall to see the great Corliss engine set in motion by President Grant assisted by the Emperor of Brazil. As the wheels began to turn the doors of all the Exhibition buildings swung open to the throngs that had gathered outside, and the Centennial Exhibition was on its way.

For the first few weeks the attendance was disappointing, but it perked up for a gala celebration of the Fourth of July which brought the greatest crowd the exhibition had up to this time enjoyed. The day was notable for two events of importance— the ringing of the new Liberty Bell, and the reading of the Declaration of Independence from the original manuscript.

The unusually hot summer was blamed for retarding the attendance seriously, and for a time it was feared disastrously; but with the arrival of autumn the "Exhibition rush" set in and brought the total close to the ten million mark. President Grant came over from Washington for the closing ceremonies and, always a man of few words, he made one of the shortest speeches of his career when he said: "Ladies and gentlemen, I now have the honor to declare the exhibition closed." He came all the way from Washington to say that.

On the instant an electrical signal connected with Machinery Hall stopped the great Corliss engine and the message, "The President has this moment closed the International Exhibition," sped by wire to all the principal cities of the world and our first centennial celebration had come to an end.

Immediately after closing day the auctioneers were called in for the greatest field-day of auctioneering the country had ever witnessed. Only the main building was to be spared, but everything else was to go under the hammer to the highest bidder. The combined cost of all the buildings had exceeded two million and a half, but the total turned in by the auctioneers came to less than three hundred thousand dollars. The Photographic Hall, which had cost twenty-three thousand, was bid in for one thousand; and the Art Gallery, costing one hundred and ten thousand, went for only three thousand. Judges Hall, built at a cost of thirty thousand, brought on the third and last call only fifteen hundred dollars; but it was the Agricultural Building which made the greatest fadeaway, for with a cost of more than two hundred and seventy-five thousand, it brought a bid of only thirteen thousand dollars. Many of the smaller and less important structures went at an even greater sacrifice, some of them being practically given away. There was some talk of a scandal and a possible investigation, but nothing came of it.

Indicative of the beginning of a fad for antiques, which had begun to make itself felt soon after the close of the Centennial, was the appearance in 1881 of a book-length poem written by Mary D. Brine under the title of *Grandma's Attic Treasures* (Dutton). Mrs. Brine was a writer of great industry during the last two decades of the nineteenth century producing thirty-four published works.

The *Attic Treasures* was a most attractive little volume of about one hundred pages containing thirty-eight woodcuts, only one copy of which is now known to be in existence. It carried a subtitle of *A Story of Old-Time Memories* and it came out at the psychological moment, for when the housewives returned home from the Centennial to their houses filled with Victorian atrocities which had driven the sound, though less ornate, furniture and household effects into the attic, they kept recalling the loveliness of that old-fashioned room at the Centennial furnished with the Putnam family relics. Then gradually, piece by piece, the colonial things began to come down from the attic and the Victorian pieces went up. It was not a complete rejuvenation, but it was a start in the right direction, and *Grandma's Attic Treasures* did the rest.

The widespread interest in the little book furnishes a fairly accurate indication of the time when the swing back to the colonial actually set in, and the long period that the book remained in print—sixty-one years—is proof positive that the interest was no mere fad but was more on the order of a trend; for the average life of an ordinary book of rustic verse could not possibly have been more than three or four years under ordinary circumstances.

The plot of the book, if it can be called a plot, has to do with a couple of city slickers who are going around the country districts buying from unsuspecting rustics for trifling sums old-fashioned and outmoded furniture and household goods which had been pushed aside as "rubbidge." It's a simple tale told by an old grandmother who sold a wagonload of her castoff furniture including grandpa's easy chair, though "a homelier thing you never did see, and plain as a pipestem too!" And there was a little old gateleg table that she had grown tired of seeing around. The slickers paid her fifty dollars for the load—and after they had gone she had a change of heart and wished she hadn't sold the things—but that came too late.

Later on she goes to the city to visit her granddaughter who had, as she said, "married riches"—and there among the potted palms, the whatnots, and the life-size sculptured Venuses on marble standards, she recognizes her dear little old gateleg table still containing the identifying marks where her children had cut their teeth on the drawer-pulls. She was "riled a mite" when she found out that the table alone had cost her granddaughter fifty dollars, the amount she herself had received for the entire wagonload; and she learns with consternation that the new-fangled things are out of style, and that now it's the old-fashioned things that everybody wants.

Here only six years after the Centennial the demand for antiques has grown so rapidly that the city auction houses are sending scouts into the country to buy the contents of the attics and storerooms of the farmhouses before the rustics discover that their pieces of "rubbidge" are in demand as antiques.

However, the fad was no fly-away craze or hobby. It was a solid growth, a development. A definite interest in antiques had come over the country, and still for the next decade or two there were not enough collectors to cause any great scarcity, not really enough to make a statistic. And the scouts sent out by the city houses did not penetrate very far beyond the suburbs. In fact, it could not be said that there was ever a real boom in antique collecting until after World War I. Just why it should have come at that particular time is not clear—but there it was.

Edwin Valentine Mitchell in his delightful book, *The Romance of Collecting*, calls it a sudden upsurge of interest. "New shops were springing up everywhere in town and country," he says. Business boomed and prices soared. The magazine *Antiques*, the first publication of its kind, made its appearance in Boston. In 1924 the American Wing of the Metropolitan was opened with its period rooms, including a number of New England interiors, and the first antique show was held in New York in 1928. By this time collecting antiques was thought to confer a certain distinction on the collector, and the ownership of fine old things became a test of social importance.

This interest in old furniture and household equipment was gravy to the country auctioneers in New England, which was and still is the American Golconda of antiques. For years the countrymen had been selling things as "good," or "used," or "secondhand," but they soon discovered that to call them "antiques" was to give them an entirely new interest and valuation. Indeed, many of them had begun to take an unwarranted advantage by describing as an antique almost any old thing that looked battered and worn. But they soon found out that many of their customers had been making a study of the subject and could tell at a glance the difference between the willow pattern of the Chinese and that of Lowestoft, and could distinguish between a Coalport glaze and a Rockingham halfway across the room.

When the crash came in 1929 many of the antique dealers shut up shop and went home for the storm to blow over, but they soon discovered that the wealthy customers hurt in the crash were anxious to sell back to them at any price they could get pieces which they had bought when times were flush, and some of the more optimistic dealers mortgaged their souls to take advantage of the bargain prices then prevailing in both city and country.

But once the market resumed after the depression it came back with the greatest upsurge it had ever enjoyed, and it is still headed in the general direction of the sky-blue yonder, as witness some of the prices being paid for French Provincial furniture and Georgian silver. There are not only more serious-minded collectors sitting in the auction rooms than ever before, but they are better informed. They read more and they talk more, both with the dealers and with other collectors.

New Englanders drift into the auction business because they are natural-born traders and love to sell things whether you want to buy them or not; and there are plenty of desirable antiques to be found in Yankeeland if you know how and where to look. I know a number of superannuated auctioneers who are leading a happy and unfettered life as free-lance antique dealers who carefully watch the unsuccessful bidders until they know who is in the market for this or that, whereupon they will pick up the article elsewhere and sell it to the loser at private sale.

But it isn't safe to express admiration for anything belonging to one of these retired auctioneers, for although his voice is gone and he is no longer on the rostrum, he will surely ask you, "What am I offered?"

CHAPTER SIX

AND SOLD TO –

THE TOBACCO AUCTIONS NOW CURRENT IN THE STATES OF THE Old Dominion date back more than three centuries into the past and still more closely resemble the country fairs of the Shakespearean period than any harvest-time festivity native to the New World. Since time immemorial, reaping the harvest has been universally regarded as an occasion for celebration as well as an opportunity to cash in on the fruits of the land, which must be harvested and preserved through the wintry months of the Temperate Zone.

Tobacco undoubtedly furnished the earliest harvest festivity of the Jamestown colonists, for it was the first money crop they ever successfully raised. They came to America with the slight misconception that the place was paved with gold. They did succeed in finding a pretty yellow metal, but when assayed it proved to be a worthless substance called iron pyrites or fool's gold. It was not until John Rolfe, the English husband of Pocohontas, discovered the secret of raising and curing the mild Virginia leaf that Jamestown made a gold strike which has since run into the millions and billions.

Indeed we are told by the statisticians that from an area in the Golden Belt of cigarette tobacco culture only twice as large as Rhode Island, growers sell their crop for millions more than the total received from the wheat crop of Kansas, the combined potato crops of Maine and Idaho, or the joint citrus crops of California and Florida.

In fact, tobacco became so valuable in Virginia that it supplanted gold and silver as legal tender. It was accepted as payment for all commodities, and even for fines and taxes. Debts and wages were paid in tobacco. Imagine peeling off a few leaves to pay a grocery bill, or rolling out a few casks to clear the mortgage from the farm. Bond servants bought their freedom with the fragrant currency. Doctors and lawyers, merchants and artisans accepted the leaf for services and goods; and undoubtedly slaves were bought and sold for a wagon-load or two.

The principal difficulty with using tobacco as money was the excessive weight. Two able-bodied men were required to roll along an average-size cask which might be needed for the purchase of a horse, a mule, or even a cow. A lesser difficulty was the bulkiness of small change in comparison with the capacity of a man's wallet.

In the early days the auction-fair was much smaller than later on, but it was invariably connected with a ball game, a parade, a wrestling match, and wound up with rollicking festivities such as dancing on the village green or strolling in the fragrant forest by moonlight. However, since the tobacco is the big feature of the day, the excitement begins with the arrival of the tobacco crop, which ordinarily starts the evening before as soon as the farmers have finished with their evening chores, and continues all through the night.

To the old-timers the scene must be reminiscent of the days when the circus used to come in over the road—the pounding of horses' hooves, the rattle of trace chains, the squeaking of leather, the crunching of iron tires over the stones, the shuffling sounds of the elephants' feet as they go lurching by in single file trunk to tail, the creaking of the gilded animal cages, and half the town out to watch the circus unload. Then one used to

smell the animals as they passed by; later the smell was the pleasant flavor of tobacco. Today there are still some hoofbeats of mules and horses, but more and more every year the sound is of horsepower and the smell is of gasoline, until one is close to the warehouse and there the fragrance of tobacco takes over once again.

It is here that the small bundles of tobacco called "hands" are sorted, graded, and piled on flat woven trays or baskets, the highest grade on one basket, the next highest on another, and so on throughout the load. Each basket is now weighed and marked with a ticket containing the name of the farmer and the weight of the load, for tobacco is sold by the pound. This information will also be recorded in the warehouseman's book at the time of sale.

The loaded baskets are now moved to their allotted places in long parallel lines extending all the way across the warehouse floor. A passageway is allowed, wide enough to permit the buyers to walk along between the rows so that they can examine closely the quality of the tobacco they are being invited to buy.

All night long the warehousemen and their clerks and helpers have been toiling at this unloading and grading task with few moments when they can stop for a brief rest, since the wagons and trucks have been waiting in line, and as one moves on another takes its place, allowing hardly a minute for an occasional coffee break when a hasty bit of refreshment can be bought from the women in gay dresses who are raising funds for the benefit of church groups or charities. And not infrequently the farmers awaiting their turns in the line will be seen dozing, for they, too, have been on the job all night.

But at last the floor is filled or the line of vehicles has come to an end, and the farmers have parked wherever they could find room and are returning somewhat nervously to await results and find out whether luck is with them or not. They realize, of course, that the auction will not start until nine o'clock, but they are drawn to the place as if by a magnet. Should the farmer be an early arrival he may still have several hours to wait, and in that case he may, after unloading, go out and look over the town, or he may roll up in a blanket and take a nap in the back of his wagon or truck.

Most of the farmers are too much excited to get any sound sleep, but they figure that even lying down will give them a certain amount of rest. However, no matter how tired they may be, they have seldom been known to oversleep unless they have had one drink too many, and that is something which almost never happens on the night before an auction. If the weather is good there is always a group waiting around the door of the warehouse from daylight on; but if it happens to be cold or rainy they go inside and stand in the aisles talking, or wander around examining the leaf that has been brought by some of the others. Many of the farmers who have been coming there for years have many friends or acquaintances with whom to discuss the weather, farm problems, prices, new babies, and obituaries.

During the early morning hours the crowd is composed mostly of farmers; but as nine o'clock approaches the buyers, brokers, and representatives of the big companies put in an appearance, and a surprising number of farmers' wives and daughters are to be seen among the crowd. Where they come from nobody knows, but there they are, some of them looking like the traditional farmers' wives only with their aprons off, and others obviously well-to-do country folk who come driving up in well-kept automobiles with plenty of pert and pretty young girls among them.

As nine o'clock approaches, the head warehouseman who has been inspecting the intake comes to the door smiling with satisfaction. "Well, boys," he says, "I reckon we've got about at least two hundred thousand pounds on the floor."

This sounds good to the crowd, and they smile and nod until a pessimist in the crowd asks, "But what about the quality?"

"Good as last year, I reckon. Mebbe bettah," the warehouse-man answers with a defiant nod of the head.

"But what about the price?" the pessimist insists.

The warehouseman laughs. "Bettah ask the auctioneer about that," he said, "Here he comes." He points with his finger at an antique Ford which comes rattling up the driveway.

"It's Jim Farnsworth!" somebody shouts. Then follows a volley of greetings.

Jim waves a hand at the crowd. "Hello, everybody!" he shouts as he leaps nimbly from his car and strides over to shake hands with the warehouseman. "How y'all been?"

"Fine, and you?"

"Nevah bettah. What kind of prospecks we-all got heah?"

"That's up to you, Jim. The warehouse is loaded, and the buyers are all ready for business."

"Okay, let's go!"

Followed by a milling throng, the warehouseman leads the way to the sales floor with the auctioneer and the buyers and brokers close behind. It is the custom for the warehouseman to set the starting price for each basket, and he picks up a hand and quickly examines it. "We'll start this lot at sixty," he announces.

The auctioneer claps his hands with a noise like a gunshot, points his finger at the first basket, and they're off. "Sixty, I hear, sixty one, one, one, two—!" His voice begins in a low chant and accelerates rapidly. So rapidly that after he reaches sixty-three the words begin to disappear. At sixty-five his voice has settled down to a low drone, and he's making only three hundred words a minute though capable of more than four hundred. There is no vocal bidding; and if there were nobody could hear it. The auctioneer's eyes are darting all over the group of customers and he catches every nod, every wink, every scratching of an ear or motion of a finger. Heaven only knows how he decides when the bidding is over, but it always comes like a flash. In this particular case it ends on the word "nine," meaning sixty-nine, and "Sold American."

There is no hammer; only a clap of the auctioneer's hands. And as a clerk picks up the tag on the sold basket a nod from the auctioneer designates the successful bidder, and on down the line he goes, with the customers scrambling along behind.

Again without a moment's pause the warehouseman gives the starting price and the auctioneer is off like a flash. The buyers, too, are now hitting their stride. They grab at the piles, haul out a hand, one quick glance and they throw it down again. If they want to bid, a glance at the auctioneer is enough. His sharp eyes are constantly alert for new bidders, and as all bids are at the rate of one additional penny a pound the bidders are all mum throughout the sale, doing all their bidding entirely by signs. Only the warehouseman and the auctioneer have anything to say, unless one of the bidders excoriates another for jostling or crowding.

As the bidding gets warmed up, the procession moves along with incredible speed, occasionally selling a basket without making a full stop, the warehouseman snatching a hand, calling an opening price, and moving on to the next basket to be ready for the auctioneer when he gets there, and the auctioneer beginning his chant before the customers are near enough to the basket to pick up the hand or even look at it.

It is really the speed of the customers that sets the pace. They are constantly jostling each other and getting in each other's way. And the faster the line moves, the rougher they are on the delicate hands of tobacco. By the time the contestants have finished the first row, tiny particles of tobacco broken from the fragile leaves are floating in the air like dust, filling the eyes with tears and smarting in the nostrils enough to cause some of those with sensitive membranes to sneeze. Truly a tobacco auction is no place for a victim of hay fever or asthma.

So rapidly do the tobacco people work, that by the time the

sale has progressed thirty yards down the line, thousands of pounds of tobacco of many different grades and prices have changed owners, and the procession now in the middle of the second line has reached a basket over which a group of brokers is having a battle royal. The evident excitement not only of the bidders, but of the auctioneer himself is attracting the crowd, which always loves a contest. The bidding is well up in the nineties before the news gets around that the battle is being fought over a basket of wrapper-leaf brought in by Eben Hill, a husky young farmer living in the neighborhood. Eben is well aware that he has brought in some premium leaf that should get him a high price. How high he could only guess, but he probably never dreamed that he would see it approaching the dollar mark.

He is patting himself on the back at ninety-five, and doing a war dance in a side aisle at ninety-eight; and when it is finally sold for a dollar he suddenly finds himself the center of a gang of dancing maniacs who nearly tear the sweat-stained shirt from his back in the enthusiasm of their congratulations.

At ninety-seven the auctioneer, despite his long experience, become so excited that he actually forgets his chant and begins pronouncing real words so that every person in the huge room is aware of the exact moment when the price goes over the top.

"I done some mighty prayin'," said Eb afterward, "but I wasn't positive-suah until I seen all that money—and there was quite a lot of it, because I had a thousand pounds of that leaf in the house."

People would be talking about Eb Hill's tobacco for the rest of the day, and possibly for the rest of the season, for dollar tobacco does not grow on every bush—not by any means.

On goes the sale up and down the aisles and up and down a diversified range of prices. A basket of almost perfect orange leaf goes for seventy-five cents a pound, and just beyond, a basket of discolored lugs brings only twenty—both raised by the same farmer on the same farm. The reason for the difference is that the lugs are not suitable for high-quality cigarettes. Only an expert could have told the difference; the fingers of a novice are not well enough educated to tell the good from the almost good; nor can the eyes of the novice read the secrets hidden in the appearance of the leaves.

As fast as the tobacco is sold it is moved out of the warehouse and taken to the buyers' "prizeries"—the factories where the leaf is packed or prized into hogsheads for shipment to the re-drying plants. The auctioneer remembers virtually every one of the hundreds of transactions of the day in spite of the speed with which he performed his services; and when the last leaf is sold and the necessity for fast talk is over, it may be noticed that he is speaking with a musical southern drawl. For a time he stands in the doorway talking with his old friends and acquaintances.

"How long you been at it, Jim?" somebody asks.

Jim gives his head a humorous shake. "Over thirty years, I reckon, first and last."

"How much ground do you cover?"

"Oh, I take in considerable territory. Start here, or in Maryland, mebbe, depending on the season, and work my way down through the Carolinas and round up through the Burley country of Kentucky, sellin' all the way, and I call it a day when I get to my home in Indiana."

"How much do you reckon you'll sell around the whole circle?"

"Well, take last year f'rinstance—my sales run up over twenty-two million pounds—and that's no guesswork, it's real figgers."

"Wow!" somebody exclaims. "That's a lot of terbacker!"

Jim nods his head. "It's quite some, specially when you remember it's sold in hunderd-pound lots."

They all stand nodding or shaking their heads until somebody asks, "What speed do you calculate to make along the floor?"

"Oh, I run along steady about six baskets a minute; but I can step it up to eight if the warehouseman is in a hurry to get home to dinner, and the buyers are spry."

"Do you reckon that chant of yours makes things go faster?"

"Well, it certainly don't slow 'em down any, but it's not primarily for speed—it's to save my voice. My vocal chords wouldn't last over four or five years if I made 'em do all the work. But with the chant your whole body gets into the act. You use your chest, your lungs, your loins, and probably your lights and your liver, too. And if I feel a little tickle in my throat, on goes a compress buttered with lard and turpentine on the inside. It's an old home remedy, but it does the business."

"But, Jim, where'd you learn to chant like that?" somebody asks.

Jim laughs softly. "Well, suh, I got the idea from an old auctioneer just as I was startin' out on my own hook. He was sorta windin' up his career and he passed it on to me as a trade secret."

"Is he still in business?" asks another.

"Oh, no, he's been dead for years, but he was an active worker for half a century, which proves that if you'll take good care of your voice it will stay with you."

"Jim," says one of the farmers, "how many tobacco auction-eers do you reckon they is all told?"

Jim chuckles. "I wrote to Washington once to find out, but they didn't know—and my guess is there's about a hunderd." He looks at his big silver watch. "I reckon I'm keepin' you folks away from your parade and pageant and all the rest of it, and I got a job waitin' for me over in the next county, so I'll be sayin'—"

The farmer catches his sleeve to detain him. "One thing more —why is it that no two terbacker auctioneers sound alike when they're both sellin' the same thing?"

"No secret about it," says Jim. "I guess it's just that no two dogs bark alike when all they're both tryin' to tell you is that there's a coon up the tree." And he gives his hat a tug and starts for his car. "Be seein' you about this time next year," he calls back over his shoulder. Then he hops aboard and goes rattling off down the driveway.

The chant of the tobacco auctioneer first came into national prominence in 1931 when it was presented as more or less of an advertising stunt on two radio broadcasts of the Lucky Strike cigarette program. It was not used regularly and consistently, however, until the latter part of 1937 when it became a regular feature of the program. During the following years different auctioneers from various sections of the tobacco country were presented, though the chant of auctioneer F. E. Boone of Lexington, Kentucky, and auctioneer L. A. "Speed" Riggs of Goldsboro, North Carolina, were heard more frequently than any of the others.

Their little ditty was taken up by newspaper columnists and comedians from whom it received much valuable publicity. Auctioneers had long been using linguistic tricks to entertain and hold the attention of their audiences and keep their interest from straying, though they never attempted anything to compare with the auctioneer's chant for the very simple reason that their bids usually came in variable amounts whereas the tobacco bids were always the same, the nod of a bidder invariably indicating a bid of one cent a pound on a hundred-pound lot.

Many years ago, before the tobacco chant had even been heard of in the North, I attended an auction in Ithaca, New York, where the auctioneer would work hard to get a bidder up to one dollar—whereupon he would burst into a chant of "one-dollar one-dollar one-dollar," spoken rapidly as long as he could exhale his breath. He did it to amuse and hold his audience, little realizing that he was also benefiting his health and saving his voice.

And only a year ago at the big strawberry auctions at Riverhead, Long Island, I listened to the chant of an auctioneer which followed the exact pattern of the tobacco auction of the South. The starting price was set by a person acting as the warehouse-man, and all subsequent bids were five cents a quart on the basis of sixteen-quart boxes per crate, and from ten to twenty crates per truck load. The initial bid was usually somewhere between four and six dollars a crate according to the variety of berry, and the bidding was done silently by blinking an eye or scratch-ing an ear, by shifting the weight from one foot to the other, by turning the page in a sales book or putting a hand in a pocket.

I thought at the time that the "elementary filler" of the chant was the word "money." But I was told by one of the truck drivers that the word was not "money" but "mama," which was probably correct, since one of the numerous auction schools in the Midwest teaches that the word "mama" chanted rapidly in a "euphonious hum" makes a highly satisfactory auctioneers' chant.

Another knowledgable authority informs us that the tobacco auctioneer uses "wah" for a quarter-cent, "hah" for half-cent, and "ree" or "rah" for three-fourths cent. "If it's tobacco that's being sold at twenty-two to twenty-three cents a pound he calls: wah-ta, wah-ta, wah-ta, hah-ta, hah-ta, hah-ta, ree-ta, ree-ta, ree-ta—and runs it off in a fast monotone."

Stuff and nonsense! At this rate it would take Jim Farnsworth some six minutes to sell one basket of Virginia leaf instead of six baskets in one minute.

CHAPTER SEVEN

THE LURE

THE BIG RED CROSS DRIVE IN EASTON, CONNECTICUT, IN THE FALL
of 1940 was really started in self-defense. Some optimist in the
higher reaches of the organization put the town down for a
quota of $700, which was a pretty big order for a community
of less than 1500 population including newborn infants, crip-
ples, and probably some cats and dogs when people were trying
to make a good showing in the census.

America was not yet in the war, but everybody else was and
we felt that we very soon would be, and certainly Easton didn't
want to be a slacker; so the local Red Cross Chapter selected the
best go-getter in town for a leader. He had recently put the
P.-T.A. on its feet and was presumably looking for new worlds
to conquer when the honor was conferred upon him.

Almost anybody else would have cried "Uncle!" and started
on a walking trip through Patagonia. But not this man. He is a
well-seasoned commuter with a business in New York, so is
accustomed to a reasonable degree of hardship. His name is
Poindexter, but for convenience I'm going to call him George,
because that's what he likes to be called.

George wasn't really very anxious for the job, but for some
obscure reason known only to himself, he took it. Heretofore
we had raised our quota by going around and ringing doorbells

and begging people for money. But George disliked the idea of begging anybody for anything. "Why not put on a big Auction Circus, and just for a change give people a chance to get something for their money?" he asked.

People raised their eyebrows slightly. This was something they had never done on a Red Cross drive. But you couldn't stop George, and he went ahead and called a meeting at which some thirty volunteers appeared. He had already selected, as his principal two associates, publisher George Brett of the Macmillan Company in New York and Mellor Jones, a crack newspaperman, both civic-minded Eastonites.

He and his two associates sold the volunteers the idea of asking residents simply to clean out their attics and send in any antiques they could find. No money this time—just antiques. Of course everybody realized that some of those attics had not been thoroughly ransacked in fifty years or more, and they retrieved some magnificent plunder.

One of the first articles brought in was a grandfather's clock which had been in one family for a century and a half; and as a proof of its quality and lasting ability, it started running when oiled and it kept excellent time. There was endless mahogany and maple, and such glassware and china as collectors dream about but seldom see. Some of it was cracked, to be sure, but to undiscriminating buyers that made it all the better.

The donations, which began to come in almost immediately, were stored in neighboring barns, and as the time for the auction approached circus tents from the old Barnum & Bailey Greatest Show on Earth were rented and set up on the Firehouse Green, and the rapidly accumulating store of goods and chattels was moved inside where it would be ready for the auctioneers and still protected from the weather in case of rain.

And in the meantime one of those miraculous coincidences which seem to follow George around had been taking place. While on a visit to New Hampshire in quest of antiques, he had met some big-game hunters who had just returned from India bringing trophies such as the skins of lions, tigers, and lesser monarchs of the jungle. One of the tiger skins had been damaged en route and George managed to get a small piece of the tail covered with fierce-looking hair. Just for a joke he tied some of this into a fishing-fly and sent it to his friend, Jack Chapman, the dramatic critic, who was in Hollywood on a newspaper assignment. He asked that Jack send him in return a lock of hair from one of the motion picture queens so that he could tie it into a trout lure to be used for publicity, and possibly sold to the highest bidder at the Red Cross auction on which he was working.

Jack, who was well acquainted in Hollywood, did better than that; he sent a lock of beautiful blonde hair contributed by Carole Lombard, and a wisp of dashing brunette which he ascribed to Hedy Lamarr. The idea of fishing for trout with a lure made of the hair of two beautiful motion picture queens appealed to George's sense of humor, and he was sitting happily at home tying on one of the Hollywood flies when his fellow conspirator, Jones, came barging in to discuss some of the angles of the publicity stories they were sending out for the auction. So occupied was George that he hardly raised an eyebrow in greeting when his friend Jones entered.

"And what are you working on so hard?" asked Jones.

George dangled the trout fly on its string. "This, my friend, and in case you don't know what it is, I may as well explain that it is a trout lure tied with a lock of hair of two of the most beautiful women in the world; you will note the blonde hair for the dark days, and the brunette for the bright ones." And he went on and told Jones with some linguistic flourishes the history of the lure.

Jones heard him out, and then began to finger the wisps of hair lying on the table. "Is this all the Hollywood hair you've got?" he asked.

George chuckled. "It's more than I need—it takes only one hook to catch a fish."

"But, my friend, we're not going to use these to lure a fish—we'll use them to lure a fisherman. What fisherman wouldn't give his right hand to cast a fly containing a wisp of hair grown personally by some of the most glamorous beauties of Beverly Hills and vicinity?"

George nodded his head. "Go on, I'm listening."

"How many lures can you make?"

"Oh—ten or twelve, I should say."

"Can you have them done by tomorrow night?"

"Easily—but why?"

"If we handle this thing right we can make a big killing. I'll get a press photographer up here to take some pictures, and I'll have the story of these flies made for the Red Cross auction in every newspaper in the country from Noank to Alcatraz, and from Niagara Falls to Tupelo."

"And how many customers will we get from either Alcatraz or Tupelo?" asked George.

"Never mind about that," said Jones. "But the entire country will know that we're having an auction. There's nothing that grabs the headlines like the hair of a Hollywood beauty. And you'll be surprised to see how the fishermen will respond to a lure of this kind. They're like fish—they'll bite on anything that resembles bait."

"And you think they'll pay five or six dollars for one of these flies?"

"Probably twice that. But that's not the catch—it's the publicity that's worth the money. We can't buy front-page space, and it would cost thousands if we could."

"And you really think we'll get it?"

"Of course we'll get it, human nature being such as it is."

"Want to bet on it?" asked George with a gleam in his eye.

"I'll do better than that—I'll eat every lure that doesn't sell under the hammer. But listen, that's on one condition—that you don't let the news leak out until after it has appeared in print."

"Can't I even tell my wife?"

"You most definitely can't tell your wife! You haven't already told her have you?"

"She knows about the tiger hair I sent Jack, but she doesn't know I've had any answer from him."

"Just don't tell her. Or if you have to lie about it, you can say you haven't heard from him yet."

George gave his head a dubious shake. "She isn't easy to lie to, but I'll try it if I have to, and I can easily get these finished before she comes home." Suddenly he cheered up. "I certainly don't want to miss a chance to see you eat a few of these lures."

Now that the atmosphere was cleared, they sat down and shaped up the story. Jones took the article and placed it where he thought it would do the most good. Just as he expected it was picked up by the big wire services and flashed all over the country, so it was seen in Hollywood and New York at the same time it appeared in the cities of New England and all over the East. It not only gave the auction a tremendous boost, but it was the laugh of the week and furnished innumerable clippings.

Getting the auction into position to function was more or less routine, but at the same time the management had plenty of surprises. They had a fleet of station wagons driven by young girls or their mothers or even their grandmothers; and while the lady drivers had to call in male help to assist with the heavier pieces, they did a highly creditable job. It was a borrowed truck driven by an incautious young woman that furnished most of the contretemps.

With the first load she brought in she collided with a center pole and knocked down one of the big tents. With the next load she managed to get the truck wedged between a large apple tree and the broad side of a barn, from which anomalous position she was rescued by a passing truck driver who nearly had

to pull the barn from its foundation to extricate her vehicle. Later on she spilled a dining-room table from her truck into a drainage ditch from which it was salvaged by a gang of telephone linemen.

There was no trouble with the station wagons. They carried tons of china and glassware without breaking a piece. Some of the glass was very rare and very beautiful, and some of it was decidedly antique. The tremendous success of the stories of the Hollywood trout lures had given the occasion such publicity as few country auctions had ever received, and from the breaking of that story until the day of the sale the telephone was ringing almost constantly with authors or volunteers who wanted to do something or give something, and autographed first editions came pouring in with every mail. People all up and down the Sound began sending in antiques by station wagon and even by truckload, and the auction management had to keep renting circus tents to put them in.

On the day of the sale there were volunteer auctioneers from all over southern New England and eastern New York. One can hardly mention any well-known auctioneer of the area who was not there.

In response to an appeal to writers for first editions of their works to be autographed on the premises and sold to the public, enough books to start a fair-sized collection were amassed, and there were times that day when so many literary folk, pen in hand, were congregated about the book section that the place needed only a few trays of cocktails to give a very lifelike resemblance to a literary tea.

However, the autograph collectors were there in such numbers that the supply of first editions was soon sold out and it was not unusual to see venturesome literary figures trying their hand as auctioneers, some of them with fairly good success. At one time the crowd stood shouting with laughter while an auctioneer who looked suspiciously like Clifton Fadiman chanted and cried and begged for some fifteen or twenty minutes before he succeeded in selling a billy goat to a Polish farmer for $9.87.

This accomplished, the handsome young literateur hurried over to the firehouse to wash the goat smell from his hands. Some of his friends caught on and kept pretending that they could still smell goat wherever he was, and he could never be quite sure that it was not so. Nobody knows how many times he washed his hands that day, but it must have been quite a number, and it would be a safe bet that he keeps no goats on his country place in Fairfield County.

Toward three in the afternoon Mellor Jones began to think about the possibility of his having to eat a few trout lures, and he started to wander around looking for anybody who had the appearance of a fisherman, for it had been mentioned in the newspapers that the Hollywood trout lures would be put on sale at that hour. He had strolled over by the firehouse where the Chief of Police was standing in the street directing traffic. Jones had just asked the chief if he had seen anyone dressed like a fisherman, when a long green Cadillac occupied by several sunburned men came to a stop and asked for parking directions. While the officer was directing them where to go another Cadillac similarly occupied drew up behind the first one. Then suddenly it dawned on Jones that several of the visitors were wearing khaki fishing hats. He went nearer and peered inside, and when he saw that one of the visitors was wearing high-top wading boots he made a bee-line for the stand where the Hollywood trout lures had been surrounded by curious crowds all day. He quickly got George's ear and told him the fishermen were coming.

"Then you won't be eating any trout lures for your supper?" George asked with a grin.

"Apparently not," said Mellor.

George had already primed his auctioneer with a special introduction guaranteeing that the Hollywood lures were genuine and were exactly as represented; and after allowing the new arrivals a reasonable opportunity to inspect the lures he gave the auctioneer the nod—and the sale was on.

The auctioneer made quite a masterpiece of his introductory remarks, reading brief selections from the sheaf of newspaper clippings he held in his hand, and when he had finished he dropped the clippings on the rostrum and took up the open box containing one of the lures. As he held it out in his hand a stillness came over the place. But at his words "What am I offered?" a dozen bids were shouted out at once. They came from all directions and in all denominations from one dollar to ten.

Fortunately the auctioneer was an old hand, and he stood smiling at the crowd until quiet had been restored. Then he said in an offhand manner, "That's better—I have a bid of one dollar."

This invited a laugh and brought the crowd to its more seemly behavior, whereupon the auctioneer asked gravely, "Does anyone make it two?"

Someone did and the bidding went on at a dollar a call. The auctioneer would hear no other figure. The contest continued until it reached fourteen dollars, and there it hung for some time until finally the man in the hip-boots made it fifteen—and it was knocked down to him.

"May I have more than one at the same price?" he asked.

And when the auctioneer said he might have as many as he wished he took one for each member of the party, and the visitors formed in line and marched up to the cashier's table. The auctioneer tried hard to get fifteen dollars for the last lure, but there were no bidders at the price, and a woman finally bought it for fourteen dollars. But she felt that she had to explain that she was buying it for her husband, not for herself.

"But why do you say that?" the auctioneer asked. "You got a good bargain."

"Well," she said, "if you must know, I don't believe any fish will ever bite on Hollywood hair."

The place was still jammed with people and several auctions were going noisily on when a local resident, a commuter who had just come in on the 3:42 pushed his way through the crowd and caught George by the arm.

"Have you sold my sofa yet?" he asked.

George shook his head. "We have no sofa of yours."

"But I left word for you to get it this morning. It's a good sofa, but we have no room for it and don't want it around."

"Do you want me to send for it?" asked George. "There's plenty of time to sell it—we're going to stay open until ten."

"I'd certainly appreciate it if you would," said the commuter.

"Sure there's somebody there?" asked George.

"Oh, yes, the maid will give it to you. Just drive right up to the side door and say I sent you."

George sent the truck for it immediately, and when it returned in half an hour he saw a very fine and very large sofa on it. Quite obviously it was not an antique, but it was a handsome piece of furniture, and people immediately began to inquire when it was going to be sold.

"I'll sell it right away," said George, "if anybody wants to bid on it."

"But it's so large," a woman customer protested. "How would anyone get it home if they did buy it?"

"We'll sell it right on the truck where it is, and deliver it to the buyer's home," said George. He called an auctioneer and the bidding started briskly. A crowd quickly gathered and had just reached fifty dollars when George felt somebody seize his arm and a voice shouted excitedly in his ear:

"Stop the sale! Stop it at once! You've got the wrong sofa—that's our *new* one—!"

George dragged the fellow away from the truck so as not to

disturb the auctioneer. "Don't get so excited," he said. "That's the one they gave us at your house."

"But that's the new one—you've got to stop the sale!"

George shook his head firmly. "But I can't stop the sale after people have begun bidding. They've established certain rights. Think I want to have a run-in with the law?"

"But, George, that's our new sofa—it matches all our new furnishings—my wife had it made to order—think I want to have a run-in with *her*?"

For a moment George was stunned. Then he thought of a solution. "I'll tell you what to do—you get in there and bid—drive the other bidders out—it's the only way!" George gave him a shove in the right direction.

The auctioneer was in full cry. "Fifty I've got—I've got the fifty—who'll make it the fifty-five?"

The owner, a tall fellow who towered above the crowd, waved his hands and bellowed, "I'll make it *sixty*—"

The crowd stopped looking at the auctioneer and gazed with open mouth at the bidder. From somewhere came a feeble bid of sixty-five, but the bidder was almost blown over by a thunderous, "Seventy-five—!"

That was the end. Nobody wanted to tangle with that fellow. The owner looked around for George, but George was diplomatically out of sight. The girl truck-driver was still sitting on the seat watching proceedings when the owner climbed up and sat down beside her.

"You heard him say he'd deliver to the buyer?"

She nodded. "I heard him. Ready to go?"

He glanced at his wrist watch. "Who loaded it for you over at my house?"

"The maid let us in and pointed out the sofa; but it was the masons working on your swimming pool who loaded it for us."

"Do you suppose they're still there?"

"They ought to be—they had a big piece of the pool to finish."

"There's still time to get this sofa back before my wife gets home. Let's go!"

When the girl truck driver came back a little later she had the old sofa on the truck. George looked at her in wonder. "How did you get that away from him?" he asked.

She smiled. "He was so glad to get there ahead of his wife that he would have given me almost anything."

"Did he say anything about paying for the other sofa?"

"Yes, he said he was going to give you an argument on it."

"I'll tell you one thing," said George, "he can't win."

"He knows that," said the girl with a smile, "and he said that if you insisted, he'd pay for it."

"Does he expect any pay for this sofa?"

"No, this is his original gift to the auction—and besides, he wants to get rid of it."

George put it on sale immediately. It brought fifty dollars.

While the Hollywood trout flies had received countrywide attention in the newspapers, it was the sale of the autographed copy of *Gone With the Wind* which aroused the greatest interest on the auction lot. The announcement from the publisher's office that there were to be no autographed copies for the public had caused quite a commotion among collectors. They were inclined to scoff at the announcement, saying that they had heard such tales before, but they had never known of a case where an autographed copy could not be obtained if the proper inducement were offered. But this case proved to be the exception.

The sales of the book had run up into the hundred thousands, and still not an autographed copy was seen or even rumored. All sorts of reasons were ascribed for the shortage but the correct one seems to have been modesty. Margaret Mitchell did not regard herself as a real author. True she had written one highly successful book, but she stated very positively that she never would write another, and she never did. While her decision was a disappointment to readers and collectors on several continents, she saved herself a tedious task that would have lasted for weeks and probably would have brought on a severe case of writer's cramp.

However, being by nature an agreeable person she compromised by autographing for her friend and publisher three copies of her famous book. Still this was a strictly confidential transaction and remained such until Mr. Brett impulsively decided to present one of the treasured copies to the Red Cross auction which was now stirring the home town to its depths. Up to this time he and the author were the only ones aware of the existence of these autographed books; but feeling that some other person should be taken at least part way into the secret, he confided to his mother the ownership of one copy, but without telling her that it was to be sold at the auction.

It so happened that when Clifton Fadiman, who was acting as auctioneer at the time, put up for sale the almost sacred opus, Mr. Brett was temporarily off the lot. He recalls that when he returned he found that the bidding on it had already reached $75. He was fascinated, he says, to find that it had gone so far so fast, and he was told that a sprightly contest was in progress between a man and a woman bidder, but his informant did not know who they were. He listened for a while where he was, then moved to a place where he could have a better view. He never did succeed in locating the man who was bidding, but the woman was easier to find, much easier, for she proved to be his own mother.

He instantly comprehended what was happening: she thought he had been carried off his feet by the spirit of the occasion and had donated to the auction the only autographed copy in existence—and now she was trying to save it for him. If that had been the case he would have been faced with quite an enigma; but since it wasn't, and the purpose of the auction was to raise money for an unusually worthy cause, he remained an amused bystander and watched his mother buy the book for $150.

Although they had been doing a land-office business all day with three and four auctioneers working at a time, antiques continued arriving about as fast as they were taken away, and by midafternoon the auction committee realized that even though they continued until ten o'clock that night there would have to be another full day's session to dispose of the property on hand. So when closing for the night, an adjournment was announced to the following Saturday, and the premises were turned over to watchmen until the next day when the surplus was put under lock and key in the barns where it had previously been stored.

The fact is that the Easton people went home that night thoroughly tired of the auction business; but by Monday morning they were rested enough to resume the work of papering the town and turning out publicity to bring the customers back for another great orgy of bargains. By this time the fine edge of enthusiasm had been somewhat dulled, but the workers plugged along doggedly hoping for the best.

To their delight and encouragement the crowds began rolling in long before the auction was ready to open, and it seemed to those in charge that the interest of the visitors was even greater than on the opening day. They were inspecting the exhibits more closely, asking more questions, peering into boxes and bureau drawers, and even pawing over the articles in the "klondikes" as the auction grab bags are called. It was George who finally discovered the cause of all this concentration, for the news leaked out that there had been a number of "finds" on the opening day of the sale.

A man who had bought a stack of old magazines for twenty-five cents found among them a Currier and Ives print worth $300; and a woman who paid a dollar for what was supposed to be a fireman's uniform discovered later that it had belonged to a Hessian soldier in the Revolutionary War and was valued at $50 and perhaps more. Then there was a smart little lady who had paid $12 for a piece of glassware believed by many people to be nothing but a funny-looking bottle, which turned out to be an antique rolling pin worth $65.

This was what came of having voluntary auctioneers who knew little about the value of real antiques, and there were any number of such helpful characters offering their services on the second day of the sale. As on the first day the place was crawling with talent of all kinds, novelists and poets, biographers and historians, painters and etchers, sculptors and engravers, along with photographers and newsmen from far and wide. There was no evening session on this occasion, and when after closing-time those in charge came together to make a brief survey of the situation, they were devastated to find that there would have to be a third session if all the property still on hand was to be brought under the hammer.

Many of the members went away disgusted, some of them muttering. And on leaving the lot not one of them spoke of the necessity of posting a watchman. A certain gentleman who shall be nameless, on being reminded by his wife on the way home that nothing had been done about taking care of the property, cheered up considerably. "Do you suppose," he said, "that there is any ethical way to let the honorable thieves of the town know about this?"

She sighed. "I'm afraid, my dear, that there are no really honorable thieves in our town; but that's not where the trouble lies. If we are ever going to escape from this trap we must stop receiving any more gifts of salable property from anybody. I think certain questionable characters are using that auction lot as a dumping ground for their junk."

Until noon the third day of the auction moved along at a fairly normal pace, but after the sun had crossed the meridian

no meandering visitor was safe from the high-pressure salesmanship which was rampant on the lot. A single bid was all that was
needed to bring down the hammer with a shout of "*Sold!*"

A bid of a dollar bought a typewriter, and five would buy a
handsome mahogany bureau or a beautiful curly maple bedstead. And by four o'clock in the afternoon the auction lot was
as bare as a newborn babe.

The original quota was $700, but the Hollywood lures raised
over $10,000 according to neighborhood hearsay. The only
trouble was that Easton could never live down so much prosperity; for the higher-ups who establish quotas could see no
reason why it couldn't be done every time.

CHAPTER EIGHT

AMONG THE OLD AND RARE

IT WAS THE EVENING OF JANUARY 28, 1947. THE PLACE WAS THE Parke-Bernet Galleries on Madison Avenue in New York. The crowd was dressed more for the Opera than for an auction, since most of the persons who had come to bid were in evening clothes with white tie and tails predominating. Even the rankest outsider who had wandered in just to get warm would have known that something big was in the offing. The atmosphere was surcharged as it often is before a thunderstorm.

People were speaking to each other in whispers and gesturing with programs and pencils. Occasionally somebody would glance around to see who was coming in, then nudge his companion and whisper in the nearest ear. This would bring a glance and a nod. The connoisseurs knew each other at least by sight, but they did not go out of their way to speak. If their eyes happened to meet they would condescend to nod slightly with a suspicion of a smile.

Nearly every person present had been over to the glass case to take a look at a little volume bound in imitation black leather with a gilt border around both covers, and a fancy scroll in the center of each. The title, *Bay Psalm Book*, also in gilt letters, appears on the spine.

The cost of such a binding today is about three dollars, but with prices what they were in 1850 it probably came to only half that much. Mr. Zoltan Haraszti, keeper of rare books at the Boston Public Library, has been quoted as saying that it would have been better if the expense of rebinding had been spared, for in that case the margins of the book would not have been trimmed by the binder.

It seems to have been taken for granted that all the prospective bidders were sufficiently well acquainted with the little volume, for it was not removed from the glass case during the auction. In the catalogue it was described as the "Crowninshield-Stevens-Brinley-Vanderbilt-Whitney" copy, the names having reference to some of the former owners, with several more entitled to be added before the evening was over.

When the auction finally began it was started with an announcement by the auctioneer that an opening bid of $30,000 had been made. There were few in the crowded room, connoisseurs or not, who did not emit or suppress a gasp of surprise. Habitués of the elite auction marts tried not to show their emotion and sat dead-pan for some moments while the more impressionable members of the audience were catching their breath and raising their dropped jaws to a normal position.

Then David Randall, representing Scribner's, who was authorized to bid as high as $90,000, and John Fleming, acting as mouthpiece for the famous bibliophile, Dr. Rosenbach, started a slow wary contest which gradually worked its way up toward $72,000 in little over half an hour. To the man of the street, if any was there, this looked like the Irish Sweepstakes; but to the initiated it began to appear as if a new record high might be going into the books, for that was the price paid by Dr. Rosenbach for a first folio of Shakespeare which had stood for fourteen years as the highest price ever paid at a public auction for a book printed in English.

But the two contestants swept right over the record as if they had never heard of it. They didn't so much as quiver when they passed the $80,000 mark, though Randall must have realized that for him the end of the line was not far away. However, as the $90,000 dollar post came into view he made a bluff at being casual as he made his bid—he must have been holding his breath as he waited to see if his opponent would go on, and Fleming quite calmly did.

Thereafter so long a pause ensued that the crowd began to think the battle was over. But this was far from the truth; it was just getting nicely started, for suddenly a new strong voice spoke up. A whisper went around that it was "Sonny" Whitney, offspring of the late Gertrude Vanderbilt Whitney, and what he said was:

"One hundred thousand dollars!"

Fleming turned slowly and looked to see who it was that had spoken. It was obvious that he was surprised, and perhaps disappointed, for he had thought the battle was won. But he came back in a strong voice with, "One hundred and one thousand."

Sonny waited a few moments, then raised the ante. "One hundred and five thousand," he said. People all around began turning and looking back at him.

Fleming came up another thousand, probably recalling that this was the exact figure at which Dr. Rosenbach had bought a Gutenburg Bible, a landmark at the time.

Sonny raised him again, this time to one hundred and ten thousand.

Fleming went up only another thousand.

"One hundred and fifteen thousand," said Sonny.

Again Fleming went up only a thousand.

This uneven bidding went on until it had reached one hundred and fifty thousand. But even though Sonny was both a

Vanderbilt and a Whitney he had a limit and had reached it when he made his bid of one hundred and fifty thousand dollars. Fleming, on the other hand, was bidding with another man's money and had only the sky for a limit, and when he raised his bid to $151,000 Sonny bowed out and Rosenbach's man got the book, though strictly speaking it was not for himself. The Rosenbach Company was acting for a group of men who intended it for the Yale Library as a gift to the University.

Higher prices have been paid for religious books, Great Britain paying $511,250 for a Bible in manuscript entitled *Codex Sinaiticus*. This was the top of the top; and in second place was the *Bedford Psalter and Hours* which had brought $165,000. As of now the *Bay Psalm Book* with its $151,000 comes third.

The first printing press came to America on the good ship *John* in September of the year 1638. It was brought ashore in the Massachusetts Bay Colony, set up in Cambridge, and put into operation by a locksmith named Stephen Daye. This locksmith-printer, feeling his way, ran through the press as his first output a one-page bulletin called the *Freeman's Oath*. Next he tried his hand on an almanac. The third job to come off his press was the *Bay Psalm Book*.

The early settlers in the Bay area had brought with them from Europe various translations of the Psalms of the Bible, and although they had long made use of the Ainsworth translations they never fully approved of them, and finally discarded them in favor of their own book of translations made by some "thirty pious ministers" of the neighborhood, of whom Richard Mather, grandfather of Cotton, was the leader. The book was a joint production of both Pilgrims and Puritans.

It was written in verse. Only 1,700 copies were printed, just enough for each family in the colony to have one. Of these only eleven copies are still in existence, and after reading a page or two, the shortage is quite understandable. Of the

eleven four are perfect, two slightly damaged, and five in-
complete. The principal value of this book lies in its scarcity,
not in its poetic beauty or literary qualities. A glance at the
Twenty-third Psalm should give some idea.

> *The Lord to mee a Shepheard is*
> *Want therefore shall not I,*
> *Hee in the folds of tender grasse,*
> *doth cause mee down to lie:*
> *To waters calm he gently leads*
> *Restore my soul doth hee:*
> *he doth in paths of righteousness*
> *for his names sake leade mee.*
> *Yea though in valley of deaths shade*
> *I walk, none ill I'l feare:*
> *because thou art with me, thy rod*
> *and staff my comfort are.*
> *For mee a table thou hast spread,*
> *in presence of my foes:*
> *thou dost annoint my head with oyle*
> *my cup it overflows.*
> *Goodness & mercy surely shall*
> *all my days follow mee:*
> *and in the Lord's house I shall dwell*
> *so long as days shall bee.*

In his fifty-five years as a book collector Thomas Prince, the
long-time pastor of Old South Church, had assembled what he
called the New England Library. In 1758 this collection, which
included five copies of the *Bay Psalm Book*, was bequeathed
to his former pastorate, Old South Church. Since this included
all five of the *Bay Psalm Books* it would appear that he must

have regarded them as having some extraneous value, for certainly they were nothing anyone would ever want to read.

The psalm books were not separately and specifically mentioned, but his will directed that *all* his books were to remain together in perpetuity—in other words forever and a day. But forever is a long time; and after remaining in the steeple chamber of the church for a little more than a hundred years, the terms of the Prince will were so far forgotten or disregarded that the library was divided, part of it going to the Massachusetts Historical Society. Forty years later, however, the two parts were brought together in the Boston Public Library where they now repose—all except three copies of the *Bay Psalm Book* which had disappeared somewhere along the way, leaving only two copies where five were shown in the original catalogue.

But to turn back to the third most costly book in the world, now very much at home in the Yale Library, and find out if we can how it managed to get there: We can't go all the way back to Stephen Daye, for it is probable that nobody knows or ever will know how Mr. Prince came to have the several copies of it in his possession. However, there must have been plenty of copies around Boston in 1703 when he was starting his library. The great question is, how did he ever come to buy so many and keep them. Was it foresight, or was it only luck? Passing this blind alley we may better inquire how the book came into the possession of Mr. Crowninshield who was listed at the auction as the first holder after Mr. Prince.

Mr. Crowninshield was a rich and exceedingly "proper" Bostonian. He was a true intellectual with exquisite taste who loved fine bindings and coveted choice books. His library was small but select. He enjoyed sniffing out rare books and going after them with diligence. It is quite possible that he may have tried unsuccessfully to buy one of the copies from Mr. Prince in person. Then after Mr. Prince's decease he may have quietly ferreted out who was in a position to dispose of a copy. And who should it be but Mr. Armstrong, a deacon of Old South Church. For many years there was a lot of mystery about the meeting between these two, for all that was known was that Crowninshield came out of it with a copy of the book. He couldn't have enjoyed his copy very much because so few people knew that he had it. After his death there was something a little furtive about the fact that his copy was not put on the market in America, but turned up in the London auction rooms of Henry Stevens who is to be remembered as the man who loved the extinct bird known as the auk, and who adopted as his telegraphic and cable address the words "Auks, London."

From the Stevens auction rooms the book was sold to George Brinley of Hartford, Connecticut, for $750. When Brinley died it went again to the auction mart where it was bought by Cornelius Vanderbilt for $1,200 and it remained in the family until the fabulous Parke-Bernet auction of 1947.

It was not until 1954 that Mr. Haraszti quite by accident made a startling discovery which threw some new light on the history of the odd little book that had made such a stir among the elite bibliophiles of the world. It was not a hunch that led him to the discovery. It was rather a curious bit of luck or if you prefer, a stroke of good fortune. While looking for something else in the vaults of the library he happened to see the little book and picked it up more out of curiosity than anything else. He was probably wondering how so small book could be worth so much money.

As he idly opened one of the two copies still in the Prince Library collection he noticed on a flyleaf something dimly written in lead pencil. His interest was aroused at once, and by holding the book carefully in the proper light he was able to decipher what was written. It was as follows:

"This book was bound at the cost of Mr. Ed Crowninshield
and given in exchange for No. 259 in the catalog.
Jan. 1850.
        "S T A"

The catalogue referred to is the first made by the Prince Library and was printed in 1846. Opposite No. 259 in the catalogue is the entry:

"The Whole Book of Psalms translated into English metre.
1640."

It takes no Sherlock Holmes to deduce that the letters "S T A" are the initials of Samuel T. Armstrong who was a deacon of Old South Church at the time the rebinding was done. He of course had access to the church library and no doubt felt that he possessed the authority to make a deal which seemed satisfactory to him and advantageous to the church. The note reads as if Crowninshield had exchanged one copy of the book for another. But such was not the case. He gave only the new binding, not the book, for the title page of the much-traveled volume still has the original shelf number it had in the library of Old South Church. All that Mr. Armstrong gained on the deal was a new binding, and a cheap one at that.

It seems quite safe to assume that Crowninshield must have been so jubilant over his big bargain that he simply couldn't keep it to himself and had to confide it to his close and intimate friend George Livermore, who was also a book collector of no mean caliber. The *Bay Psalm Book* was right up his alley, for his taste ran to books of a holy or sacred character. He had a large collection of Bibles which had belonged to prominent persons, especially noted divines. His sketch in the *Proceedings of the Massachusetts Historical Society*, the bluebook of Boston aristocracy, covers more than fifty pages with a liberal sprinkling of such words as "intellectual," "philanthropic," "ardent," "illustrious," "intelligent," "exquisite," etc.

Of course the inevitable happened. It was just too easy to pass up, and soon a copy of the *Bay Psalm Book* appeared on the shelves of Mr. Livermore's library, and a cheap new binding was to be found on a second *Bay Psalm Book* in the library of Old South Church. Mr. Livermore had to take an imperfect copy from which several leaves were missing, and he did not hesitate to trade away several other leaves, which cheapened the value of his copy, for when it went under the auctioneer's hammer after his death it brought only $425, but after all 99 per cent of the intake was profit. This copy is now in a private collection in Brooklyn.

It was not long before another collector, Dr. N. B. Shurtleff, had the good fortune to discover that the Crowninshield and Livermore copies had been wheedled out of a deacon of the church, and he determined to try his hand at wheedling. But being too busy with his practice and his politics—he was three times Mayor of Boston—he sent in his order by mail. There was no finesse about that fellow, but he was a good trader. He wrote that he had a "strong veneration" for the old book and would like to acquire one of the "duplicate" copies, offering in exchange "original editions" of two books which he happened to think would be of great value to the Old South Library. This from the ex-Mayor of Boston himself! The deacon, utterly overwhelmed, surrendered to the doctor a choice copy which had been owned, and autographed on several pages, by none other than Richard Mather, one of the coauthors of the book, and it is quite likely that the deacon apologized for the fact that it was a used copy.

The two books which the deacon received in exchange, Winthrop's *New England,* and Belknap's *New England Biography* were probably worth together no more than five or six dollars, and what that autographed copy of the *Bay Psalm Book* would bring if placed on the auction block today is just nobody's business.

In his glee over making the exchange of two cheap books for one invaluable rarity Dr. Shurtleff decided that an inscription might add some elegance to the occasion, so he wrote in each volume the inscription, "Given to the Prince Library of the 'Old Church Society' of Boston, Mass., by Nathaniel B. Shurtleff, M.D., in exchange for the 'Bay State Psalm.' [Not even the correct title!] Boston Jan. 11, 1860."

Dr. Shurtleff, though a prominent citizen in a political way, was by no means so "proper" as either Crowninshield or Livermore in an aristocratic way. He still had the treasured copy of the *Bay Psalm Book* when he died in 1874. The deacon seems to have been lost by the wayside, and whatever it may have been that stirred the officials of Old South Church to action some twenty-five years after the fact can only be guessed at. There may have been some posthumous publicity about the doctor's collection of books; or it might have been the inscriptions in his own handwriting that furnished documentary evidence of a fraudulent deal; but in any event when, upon Shurtleff's death, his library was offered at auction by Leonard & Company of Boston in November, 1875, the *Bay Psalm Book* was withdrawn because the deacons of Old South Church had obtained an injunction to prevent the sale. However, the injunction was dissolved after a court hearing and the book adjudged to belong to the Shurtleff estate on the ground that the suit was barred by the statute of limitations.

So the book was again offered at auction with an impressive four-page circular and was bought by Mr. Sidney S. Rider of Providence, Rhode Island, for $1,025. From Mr. Rider the volume passed to Mr. Caleb Fisk Harris, and upon the death of Mr. Harris in 1881 it reached a permanent resting place in the John Carter Brown Library at Brown University.

The entire Crowninshield Library was sold to the ubiquitous Henry Stevens at private sale for $10,000, and Mr. Stevens had the astonishing experience of having his copy of the *Bay Psalm Book* refused by the British Museum though offered for only £150. Later he sold the copy to Mr. George Brindley of Hartford for 150 guineas, then worth about $750.

It is interesting to note that the original sale price of this, the third most valuable book in the world, was 20 pence a copy.

Book collecting as distinct from the formation of working libraries is said to have begun in England as a reaction from the book massacres when the monasteries were dissolved by Henry VIII, and the college and university libraries were stripped and plundered, the main object of book collecting at that time being to rescue good books from perishing. Now in a world where good books no longer need rescuing, the emphasis is on those which are old and rare—and the older and rarer they are the higher the prices they command until book collecting has become to a large extent a rich man's fancy.

Occasionally a born collector who simply cannot go wrong will come out of the nowhere. The brilliant success of Jerome Kern as a book collector undoubtedly started hundreds of the young people of the theater collecting first editions and spending their slender means in the secondhand stores on worthless tomes, simply because they looked old enough to be rare. Jerome Kern was already a musical genius with a flare for light verse and an ample income from his royalties before he ever collected a book. He was also a shrewd buyer and an expert salesman, and if he ever went wrong on one of his purchases nobody knew about it; and in some fourteen years he amassed a collection, the sale of which in March of 1929 became the literary sensation of the twenties and was everywhere regarded as second only to that of Robert Hoe III, which had held the center of the book-collecting stage in America since 1911.

The Kern sale came during the period of the great bull market when people had become accustomed to talking not only of two chickens in every dinner pail, but of two automobiles in every garage. Everybody was making a lot of money and spending it freely, and it looked as if the prosperous times had come to stay.

Prices for the old and rare books were flying high. A first edition of *Tom Jones*, purchased a few years before at $3,000, went to Dr. Rosenbach under the hammer for $29,000; and Shelley's own copy of *Queen Mab* with the poet's personal manuscript revisions went sailing skyward from $12,000 to $68,000, although in 1920 it had been sold at the Buxton Fore-man auction for only $6,000.

There were other instances of the same kind too numerous to mention, and book-dealer Gabriel Wells was blustering around declaring that the books he had sold to Kern in the past few years had brought the canny collector $345,000 more than they had cost him. It was said editorially that the book-collecting game had become a "twentieth century frenzied finance." The total amount of the 1,482 items of the Kern sale realized $1,729,462, or an average price per volume of $1,167 ranking it next to the Hoe collection as the second most valu-able ever sold on this continent up to that time. But we must remember that the Kern sale had been held only a few months before the big crash of 1929; and when *Queen Mab* was in the headlines again along in the thirties it was sold as part of the literary stock of Gabriel Wells Bookshop at the Parke-Bernet

Galleries for only $8,000—a loss of some sixty thousand dollars on a single book—but not while it belonged to Kern.

Hoe, on the other hand, was not a merchandiser, but a real booklover who had spent some fifty years amassing his beloved collection, whereas Kern, though fame came to him as a talented composer, was even more talented as a trader, a merchandiser. His head was never in the clouds. He could cope easily with Tin Pan Alley and had made a sizable fortune there before he took up book collecting as a remunerative side line. In less than fifteen years he had made a million and three-quarters out of his rare book hobby and was still receiving munificent royalties from the Alley.

Hoe had been in his grave for six years before Kern ever bought a book as a speculation. The opening sale of the Hoe collection had taken place at the Anderson Gallery in April, 1911. It was indeed a gala occasion with booksellers and collectors gathered from all over the world. Kern himself may easily have been in the audience, for it was the place to be on that particular evening. Among others, Henry E. Huntington was represented there, and as usual Miss Belle da Costa (Greene) was on hand as the stand-in for J. P. Morgan.

It was quite obvious that a new scale of prices had arrived when a second edition of *Bacon's Essays*, which had on its last appearance grudgingly brought $160, was quickly bid up to $1,575. There were some sparring matches between the Huntington and the Morgan forces before the sale had progressed more than a few minutes, but the first real tug of war came at the next session when Huntington acquired the *Book of St. Albans* for $12,000, and a Gutenberg Bible on vellum at $50,000, a new high at the time, though the vellum edition has by the present time passed the $100,000 mark and even the paper version has doubled in value. There were two editions made by Gutenberg, the first with pages containing forty-one, forty-two, and forty-three lines to the column, doubtless for experimental purposes; the second with the same number of lines on every column, forty-two.

Despite the popular belief that there is only a single Gutenberg Bible in existence, there are now forty known copies, and it is not impossible that others may still be found. Indeed a second Gutenberg Bible, this one printed on paper, went at the Hoe sale for $27,500.

There was another battle royal over a Malory translation of *Le Mort d'Arthur* printed by Caxton in 1485. This went to Morgan for $42,800 after a spirited contest—a decided accretion for a book which had previously sold at auction for 62 cents. Part I of the sale realized a total of $997,363, more than half of which had come from the well-filled coffers of Mr. Huntington.

The immediate reaction from the Hoe sale was that the outrageously high prices could not help having an adverse effect on the rare book business, one of the disappointed dealers complaining that he had orders to bid on some three hundred items, but was unable to realize on even one.

The first edition of the Lewis Carroll masterpiece was issued in 1865 under the title of *Alice's Adventures in Wonderland* with the well-known illustrations by Sir John Tenniel. But the first handwritten manuscript remained in the hands of Mrs. Hargreaves, who was little Alice grown to womanhood. She held it until 1928 when she felt herself obliged to sell it to permit her to live in comfort until the end of her life. It was auctioned off at Sotheby's April 3, 1928, to Dr. Rosenbach for $75,259.80.

But the British were feeling so downcast over their loss that Dr. Rosenbach assured them through the press that he would resell the volume to them for exactly what it had cost him, though he had been prepared to pay $100,000 for it. However, the Museum couldn't raise the money, and the manuscript went back to America in the Doctor's portfolio, but not to stay.

For the time came when some generous-hearted American started a campaign to raise a fund for the purpose of sending the keepsake back to Britain where it belonged. Many, many persons made contributions, but it is said that Dr. Rosenbach's donation was the largest of all. And now if the Americans want to see the original source manuscript from which the story of Alice grew they must go to the British Museum. Contrariwise, they must go to Havana, Cuba, to see the fifth holograph draft by Lincoln of the Gettysburg Address for which the late Señor Oscar B. Cintas, a Cuban collector, paid $54,000.

CHAPTER NINE

HUDSON VALLEY COWPUNCHER

ARGYLE, NEW YORK, IS A NEAT, CLEAN LITTLE ONE-STREET town not far from the center of Washington County. It was settled by a group of sturdy Scots from Argyllshire long enough ago for them to have taken part in the Revolutionary War, but it still speaks with an unmistakable burr. It lies near the center of a rolling terrain that is probably the finest cattle country in the state of New York. A mile or two south of the village on a gentle westerly slope toward the Hudson River is a stately white mansion set in a towering grove of elms and maples across the road from a large conglomeration of barns, sheds, pens, and other buildings—including a lunchroom. In front of the buildings is an acre or more of blacktop pavement. The place had a look that was so decidedly official that I would have thought it was some kind of county or municipal organization had it not been for the animal odor that pervaded the atmosphere. It was no ordinary barnyard setup. I was sure of that because everything in sight was painted, scrubbed, and polished until it shone like a new pair of shoes.

"This is the place," said my companion, a resident of nearby Hudson Falls.

"It can't be," I protested. "Look at the cars parked in the driveway. Do auctioneers drive around in Cadillacs, Lincolns, and Thunderbirds?"

"Could be," he said, "for there's Mr. Miller just coming out of the big barn."

We parked our car on the pavement and went over and made ourselves known. Mr. Miller, a tall, well-built man with a healthy tan and a keen eye invited us into his office which was one flight up a broad staircase in the barn. It was such an office as might have been found in any prosperous country bank. Indeed it looked very much like a bank, with a long stand-up desk with several wickets through which customers could be waited on. There were no chairs in the general office. This gave the impression of being cleared for action.

We had previously discussed over the telephone the purpose of my visit so I went right along with my questions. "How long have you been in auctioneering?" I asked.

"I started about fifteen years ago."

"How did you happen to take up the business?"

"Well, I always liked it, and I thought that if the other fellow could make a go of it, I could."

"And how did you get started?"

Mr. Miller pushed his hat to the back of his head. "About the first thing I did was to go to an auctioneering school."

"Fair enough," I said. "Where did you hang up your shingle?"

"I started in at the old Farmers' Sheds in Glens Falls, selling farming implements and some livestock."

"Were you scared the first time?"

"Not in particular."

"How did you make out?"

"That first auction got me started, and in time I launched out as a general auctioneer."

"You sold furniture, household effects, all kinds of personal property, as well as farming equipment and animals?"

"That's right."

"Did you come across any antiques?"

"Not too many. I like antiques, and I like the idea of selling them, but we don't seem to have a great many in this area. I never got hold of much period furniture, antique glass, or any very valuable silverware."

"Then you never got anything that 'came over on the *Mayflower*,' or even a Paul Revere pewter porringer?"

"Not that I know of."

"How about paintings? Ever get hold of an old banged-up picture that turned out to have been painted by one of the Old Masters—after somebody had bought it for a couple of dollars?"

"I'm afraid not. The nearest I ever came to that was when somebody else found an old Currier and Ives up here at Argyle that they say was sold for $1,250."

"What about fancy breeding—don't the farmers around here go in for registered livestock?"

Mr. Miller shook his head. "Not the real farmers who work for a living, but just the gentlemen farmers who do their farming for fun."

"How about the horse auctions at Saratoga?" I asked.

"But those are race horses like Swaps and Seabiscuit," he protested. "The farmers may go over to see the horses run, but they don't bring many of them back with 'em. If I'm going to make any money here, I have to do a volume business. My sales here are all on a commission basis. No sales—no commission. So I have to hustle."

"And the sky's the limit?" I said.

"Not quite," he answered. "We're limited by the amount of stock we can put through our plant in a day. A while back we had a peculiar situation around here. The farmers had no market where they could sell their surplus stock except to the roving buyers who used to come around looking for bargains. A good many of them were shady characters who would beat a man down as low as they possibly could. They wanted all the profit for themselves, and the farmers could do no better than take whatever they offered. It wasn't as if they had competitive bidding with a hundred or a thousand buyers looking on, any one of which might speak up and make an offer.

"That's the kind of a setup we have today. When a farmer brings in an animal to sell, he's practically certain to get a fair value for his beast, for he gets the entire price—with the exception of the reasonable commission we charge. We make a steady market for him, and that's the way we have built up our big volume."

"You spoke about that once before," I said. "Would you feel like telling me what your annual volume is likely to amount to?"

"I certainly would," he said. "I keep close track of my figures, and so far this year our turnover had been over a million and a half, and with the best part of the year still ahead—we'll certainly go over two million—by quite a little margin I expect."

I must have gasped audibly. "Do the farmers realize that?"

"I don't know why not," he said. "All they've got to do is take a lead pencil and do a little arithmetic."

"But isn't that big business for a rural setup?"

"Sure it is. But we cover a big territory of the most productive cattle country in the state. We hold an auction every week on Wednesday, week in and week out, all the year, summer and winter. Our largest attendance is in the fall and winter because there's less work for the farmers to do. It's hard to keep an accurate count because some of the farmers are moving in and out all the time; but our average must be some-

where around 500. On some special occasions we must have
had over 2,000.

"The stock begins coming in about eight o'clock in the
morning, and from that time until six or seven that night there
will be a line of trucks unloading at the calf pens, for we sell
about 650 calves at every auction."

I was inclined to take this with a grain of salt. "How many
do you sell at a time?" I asked.

"Only one. They all belong to different people and they're
all mixed up."

"What time do they go on sale?"

"Two o'clock sharp."

"And how long does it take you to sell a calf?"

"Not long—I can sell about fifteen a minute."

I could feel my jaw slipping a bit. "And you mean to tell me
that you can sell fifteen individual calves to fifteen individual
buyers in one single minute?"

"Some of the buyers may buy more than one, if that's what
you mean, but there will be at least fifteen separate sales."

"But, Mr. Miller, how can you do that?" I insisted. "Is it
another case where the hand is quicker than the eye?"

He laughed comfortably. "There's no trick about it, it's
entirely a matter of skill. Come around tomorrow at two o'clock
and I'll show you how it's done."

I turned slowly and looked at my companion. "How about
it?"

He nodded his head positively. "We'll be there," he said.

"Fine," said Mr. Miller. "And now wouldn't you like to take
a look at the ring, the arena, and the rest of our equipment?
It's empty just now but there will be plenty going on there
tomorrow."

We were quite agreeable to his suggestion and in his company
we walked along the broad hallway a few steps and on opening

a door found ourselves looking down from the gallery of an arena with a seating capacity of considerably over a hundred and standing room for many more. In the middle of the stage was an office containing a pulpit for the auctioneer, a desk for the clerk, and a loud-speaker for the hard-of-hearing.

At the left was a spotless platform scale large enough to weigh an elephant or a yoke of full-grown oxen. In front of the stage where an orchestra pit might have been expected was a straw-covered space nearly big enough to accommodate the Philharmonic or a small herd of yearlings which are usuallly sold in a group, we were told. The beef critters are sold by the pound as they step off the scale which, in addition to indicating the weight on a gigantic dial visible all over the arena, avoids all chance of error by issuing a printed weight ticket.

Dairy cattle and budding yearlings depending for their value on their lacteal possibilities are quite naturally sold individually, the yearlings starting as low as $50 while the milkers begin around $100 and often considerably more. The bulls are spotty, I understand, the starting point depending largely on disposition and their social behavior while in the ring.

As the hammer comes down on the final bid in the ring the selected one is hustled out on one side as the new candidate is boosted in on the other side. And this goes on until the holding pens are empty and the outgoing pens are full.

Next day when my companion and I returned to the Miller farm for the auction, we encountered such a tangle of trucks and other traffic that we found ourselves compelled to park in an open meadow far from the scene of action. Lines of trucks had already formed along the road, one leading to the calf pen and others to the various enclosures where beef cattle, bulls, hogs, and even sheep and goats were being unloaded.

We found the main calf pen jammed almost to the point of suffocation, and I was astonished to note that out of some two

hundred calves in the pen all but two were black and white
Holsteins, the two little exceptions being red Guernseys—and
this proportion held all through the rest of the day. The calves
appeared to have enjoyed their truck ride, for most of them
were reluctant to get out on the ground and had to be hauled
out by a hind leg or by the tail, though the conventional hold
for propelling a calf after it had been grounded was to hustle
it along by gripping the left ear and the tail and making it
"walk turkey," usually bawling with fright after the right ear
had been tagged, this being the regular tagging place.

For a while we watched the handlers putting on the tags as
they shouted out the number and the name of the farmer so
proper entry could be made in the record. Usually there were
several calves in each truck, and all after being tagged and
entered were crammed into the big receiving pen. No matter
how crowded the pen became the handlers always assumed that
there was room for one more—and apparently there always was.

Then suddenly the door into the calf house was opened and
a flood of calves gushed through the doorway and into the
building, all of them crowding and many of them bellowing.
They found themselves in an inside pen which converged into
a chute along which they were pushed by forces from behind
and hauled by handlers up in front, who now propelled them
into a narrow aisle between the two sides of a small grandstand
on which sat opposing lines of calf-buyers holding pads and
pencils in their hands. At the head of the double row stood
the auctioneer with a three-foot stump of an old rattan whip
in his hand. Seated on a platform at his shoulder with a large
loose-leaf record book sat a checker who jotted down the
number of the calf as it was called aloud, and the name or initials
of the buyer when it was bought.

The calf was scared and bawling as he was sent flying along,
and his number, 390, went right along with him, each handler

who touched him shouting the number. Standing beside the checker I saw him write the figure down and enter the initials B.S. beside it.

I could hear the low-voiced chant of the auctioneer as he waved his whip back and forth from one side of the grandstand to the other. But suddenly I noticed that the calf was gone and the checker was jotting down $6 and another set of initials, as well as a new number. Then I realized that the chant was practically continuous and that the calves were being sold as they went skidding past without even coming to a full stop. A glance at the checker's book confirmed this, for he was steadily entering new numbers, new prices, and new initials while I had not been able to translate a word of the chant, nor had I heard anybody make a bid. It just did not make sense to me though it apparently did to everybody else, and especially the checker who sat calmly on his high seat and didn't even seem to be in a hurry. Why, once when a calf fell down and momentarily interrupted the line I saw the checker lighting a cigarette.

With all the confusion, the shouting of numbers, and bawling of calves, I simply couldn't hear myself think and was rapidly approaching a state of incomprehension when another calf fell down and the handler fell on top of it, and another calf coming up from behind started to climb up on the fallen handler's back. There was an outburst of laughter as the line came to a sudden stop and I took advantage of the pause to ask the checker, "How can you tell when they bid?"

"Watch the whip," he said from the corner of his mouth as the assembly line was starting to move again.

I did watch the whip and soon discovered that the man at whom the whip was pointing was the one who had made the last bid. I next discovered that no two bidders used the same sign, one raised a finger of the hand resting on his knee, another winked an eye, and still another gave a slight nod of the head. But it was fast work; if there wasn't another sign within a tick of the clock the whip came down and the buyer's name was called.

Then I discovered another thing—the starting point was always given by the auctioneer himself and each bid meant a raise of fifty cents. Now I felt that we were ready to do some timing. My companion held the watch to keep track of the seconds while I kept count of the calves that went by. "Go!" he suddenly whispered in my ear, and I began to count. In what seemed like an age he gave me a poke and whispered, "Stop— the minute's up!" He held up his watch. "How many?" he asked.

"I counted sixteen," I answered dubiously, "but it couldn't possibly have been right. Either I counted wrong, or you must have gone longer than a minute."

"My count was perfect," he insisted. "I never took my eyes off the second hand during the entire time."

"But that's less than four seconds per calf," I protested. "It couldn't be right. Let's try again."

We did, several times, and while the count never went to sixteen again it touched fourteen and fifteen several times. We found later on when the official count was taken that 715 calves were sold that afternoon. And just to show that the auctioneer was not loafing on the job he sold 252 beef cattle that same day, 13 bulls, 10 dairy cows, 16 hogs, and 48 sheep and lambs.

The auction lasted until eleven o'clock that night, and total sales for the day were up in the forty thousands. And although it is the boast at Miller's that any farmer may have his pay twenty minutes after the sale is made, the number of checks mailed out that night to farmers who had neglected to pick up their pay numbered 573.

However, it was two-thirty in the morning before the office

force consisting of four girls and a boy wearily turned out the lights and started for home.

It is probably just as well that the auctions come only once a week, for I don't see how any human voice—even with the saving grace of the magnificent Miller chant—could thrive with more than one such experience a week. But the truth is that Mr. Miller takes on an occasional auction that has no connection with his work among the livestock. And he has even been known to take a flyer in some "asinine business," as one of his friends humorously alludes to his venture in the sale of Mexican burros.

Nobody knows how the craze for burros began; but instead of asking Dad for a bicycle, Junior began teasing for a Mexican burro. Quite understandably Dad said No very firmly. However, as burros began to show up here and there and Dad became accustomed to seeing them around, his No became less and less positive. Then finally, in a moment of weakness he asked Mr. Miller if he had any burros for sale.

As it happened, Mr. Miller didn't, but after a number of other fathers had asked him the same question he began to consider the matter.

Then he wrote to a friend in Witchita, Kansas, and it so happened that the friend had a friend in Mexico who was thoroughly familiar with the burro business. The result was that a carload of burros was soon on its way to the Miller farm. Seven days later, to the astonishment of the station agent at Schuylerville, N.Y., a cattle car packed with Mexican burros was shunted to his siding and left there. When the burros began to ask for their breakfast the station agent quickly summoned the Miller farm by telephone to come and get them. And then the fun began.

Mr. Miller ran advertisements in the newspapers of all the surrounding towns. Then he borrowed an idea from the burros themselves, who are famous for their word-of-mouth advertising; he put a baby burro in the back of a car equipped with

a loud speaker and made a thorough coverage of most of the
towns in the upper-Hudson watershed, inviting the public to
an opening exhibition of the little Mexican songsters the following Sunday. Usually it was the driver who extended the invitation, but occasionally the little burro would be heard from.

For instance, as they were passing through Glens Falls they
were fortunate enough to be stopped by a red light in the very
center of the city—and that was the moment when the baby
burro stretched out his neck and let loose a prolonged Mexican
Hee-haw! which aroused the population for blocks around.
People came rushing to the doors of the stores and peered out.
It even woke up the traffic cop who was dozing on the corner.

Sensing a violation of the rules of the road, the officer blew
a sharp blast on his whistle and came striding over to see who
was making all the commotion—but when he saw the little baby
burro he stopped short in his tracks, spit his whistle out of his
mouth, and when the burro sounded his high note the copper
answered with a hearty "Haw-haw!" Probably the inhabitants
had never seen that cop laugh before, and they too began to
laugh and chortle and cheer. And then the light changed and
the loud speaker moved on with a cordial invitation to one and
all to come over on Sunday and get acquainted with the rest
of the carload.

It would seem that everybody came, for the Miller parking
space, the roadside for half a mile or more, and even the open
fields were so jammed with parked vehicles that policing was
practicably impossible, and urchins, both boys and girls, were
scrambling over the low fences of the exhibition pen and steal-
ing burro rides, often with two and sometimes three riders
aboard, "ridin' 'em raw," as one of the old stable hands remarked, "without no bridle, and not even a saddle on the ass."

"We hadn't intended to offer any of them for sale that day,"
Mr. Miller explained, "but visitors kept asking the prices, and
when the crowd finally thinned out that day there weren't

many of the little fellows left. I remember one lady asked me the price of a certain burro and when I told her $150 she said it was too much and walked away; but a man standing nearby asked the price of another burro and when I told him $250 he said he'd take them both, and by golly he did. Then in a little while the woman came back and said she had changed her mind and I had to tell her she was too late. She was terribly disappointed."

"Did you ever sell any more burros?" I asked.

"Yes, two more carloads," he said. "But after all, we had no ambition to go into the burro business. We realized that while they are nice little animals for children to have for pets, they were only a fad, and would in time go the way of all fads; whereas, the good old cow and calf, the beef stock, and the dairy herd would go on forever.

"So we raised our sights, enlarged our plant, and now that my son is out of the Service we're doing very nicely, thank you."

COUNTRY AUCTIONEER

WITH THE COMING OF THE TWENTIETH CENTURY THE SOCIAL position of the auctioneer was about on par with that of a book agent or lightning-rod salesman; and the reputation of the ordinary city auctioneer was far more unsavory than that of the country or small-town operator, though the general impression was that all of them would bear watching.

For a crook to pass as a respectable citizen in the country is much more difficult than in the city. The country folk know too much about other people's business for a cheat or trickster to go long undiscovered, and if a person, be he yokel or villager, gets gypped he tells the world and soon the perpetrator is on everybody's black list. Of course there are some shady characters in the auction business just as there are in the pulpit or the Y.M.C.A. Secretariat; but today the great majority of going-going-goners are as honest as the average politician or plumber. Not only have they found that a reputation for honesty is a prime asset in the auction business, but a large proportion of the operatives now come from the upper-middle class, or possibly from the underlevel of the upper class where business dishonesty is no longer respectable or even profitable. While there are no reliable statistics on the subject, it is quite obvious to the casual observer that the number of retired personnel, both men and women, now engaged in conducting antique shops in the country is legion.

The training required for such self-employment is practically nil. It usually begins by attending auctions, quite a good many auctions, perhaps merely as a form of entertainment. Gradually the interest grows. The victims begin to know a Hitchcock chair from a fiddleback, a Duncan Phyffe from a Heppelwhite, a Queen Anne from a Chippendale, and a comb-back round-about from a Philadelphia stick. They come to understand that milk glass does not come from cows any more than Sandwich glass is good to eat. Little by little they become alert to the prices brought by this and that, and they begin to borrow and read a few good books on antiques.

After that comes a period of low-price collecting, and when they have assembled enough to make a respectable showing they hang out a homemade sign, put on a pair of horn-rim spectacles —and there you are!

It's nice to have a little business of your own if your social security plus your retirement pension is not quite enough for you to live on. And if your antique collection is too small to support a shop you can easily pick up a bit of commission business from the neighbors, for almost every old house in the country can produce a few broken-down chairs, cracked lamps, and nicked glass and china as well as other discarded rubbish that has been cluttering up the pantry shelves or gathering dust in the attic for you don't know how long. And if you have a good voice and an ample supply of old jokes it is only a short step from the antique dealer to the rostrum of the auctioneer.

Thirty years ago there was only one auctioneer in the entire township of Monroe, Connecticut, and he had so little call for his services that in his spare time he successfully operated a hundred-acre farm from which he made a good living. If you should go to interview him today you would find him hale and hearty although in his youthful seventies. His hair is white, but most of it is still with him. He is quite a little larger in the middle than at either end, and he shows every evidence of having lived well. He has the satisfied air of a man who has had a good life and who doesn't mind telling about it. His story would go something like this:

"Yes, I been an auctioneer quite a while. Don't recollect the exact date when I started, but I kept at it for more'n forty years before my voice finally give out and I had to quit and retire. Got into the business by a sort of an accident. I was naturally an accommodatin' feller, and several times when they had a lot of pies and cakes left over at a church sociable the women folks would ask me to sell 'em, and just for the fun of it I would cry 'em off like an auctioneer and I could always sell 'em. Got good prices, too. In fact I turned out to be so good at it that a friend of mine who was made executor of an estate come around and asked me to auction off a house full of furniture and other personal effects left by the late deceased.

"Some of the relatives was a little nervous when they heard I had the job. They thought I couldn't do it. But the executor insisted and I went ahead with it. Sold everythin' upstairs and down, cleaned it all out to the last sliver—and that's how I made my start as a regular paid auctioneer.

"I never claimed to be much of an appraiser and I never would estimate in advance what the goods and chattels ought to bring. My notion was that any article was worth whatever folks was willin' to pay for it. That's been my policy all along, and it worked.

"I've had a lot of thrills in my day, and I've had some comical things, too. I guess the crowd got the most laughs out of the time when I sold a lot of ladies' undergarments that had belonged to a deceased actress. They had been put away in the draws of a big old bureau that was up for sale. There wasn't any near relatives to interfere, so the executor decided to put 'em right into the sale. I didn't really know what was there. Hadn't given more than a glance into one of the draws and about all I saw was some bed linen and towels that was right on the top. Household linens always go well at an auction, and the upper draws where they was emptied in no time at all.

"So my helper dug into one of the lower draws and the next thing I knew my hands was full of ladies' underthings with lace and ruffles on 'em and pink and blue bows and ribbons peeping out. Right off I suspected these things of being a little too intimate to be showing in mixed company, and I tried to slip them back to him. But he was bent over and wasn't lookin' my way. So I tried to shove them out of sight and announced that the contents of the lower draws would go with the bureau.

"I still think it was a good alibi and I believe everythin' would have been all right if it hadn't been for a nosy woman in the front row who stood up and cried out, 'But we want to see what's in 'em! Show us what you've got there!'

"By this time the audience had caught on and they were stretchin' their necks and laughin' and callin' out from all sides, 'Let's see 'em—let's see 'em!'

"Now I want to explain right here that this happened some time ago. It was before the women had challenged the man's divine right of wearin' visible pants. What they might be wearin' underneath their skirts was their own business and somethin' certainly not intended to be displayed at an auction. And yet here was the women themselves insistin' that I should show up these intimate undergarments before an audience with almost as many men as women. It makes a feller wonder.

"An auctioneer knows fairly well how to handle an audience, and when I saw those women so headstrong about it I decided to give them a good show. So I took out the top article and held it up in front of my body for all to see—and it brought the biggest laugh I ever drew in all my forty-odd years of auction-

eerin'. It was several minutes before the crowd become quiet
enough for me to go on with the biddin', for what I had showed
'em was the laciest, raciest, most beribboned pair of lady's
unmentionables you could ever imagine.

"And the fun lasted long after I got the biddin' started.
Seemed like ever'body in that room wanted to bid on every
pair I put up. The bids come so fast I simply couldn't keep
track of 'em. Men and women alike were wavin' their hands
and frantically shoutin' out their bids like a lot of Wall Street
lunatics tryin' to corner the wheat market. It was prob'ly the
most hilarious auction ever held in New England. No tellin'
how high the biddin' would have gone if I hadn't put a gag on
it; and when I thought the price on an article had gone high
enough to cause a scandal—I'd just bring down my hammer and
declare it sold.

"I understand there was quite a little speculation afterwards,
and some kiddin' amongst the masculine bidders about how they
had disposed of some of the things they had bought, especially
the restless husbands with plain-lookin' wives interested mostly
in church work.

"Can't recollect any other experience with fancy underthings, but I will say that first and last I've sold a lot of reg'lar
clothes under the hammer. Overcoats and furs was easy to sell,
but ladies' dresses and men's suits had to be just so or they
wouldn't go at all. Flashy things easy to remember wouldn't
hardly get a bid. For some reason folks don't like to have it
known that they're wearin' castoffs of somebody else. But you
take plain clothes hard to identify, and believe me they'll buy
those.

"Another thing they'll bid on is any old kind of uniform,
especially if it's got brass buttons on it. Don't matter if it's all
riddled with moth holes so long as the buttons are the original
brasses. Sometimes it's hard to tell why people bid on useless

things, and yet they will do it. Take the old-fashioned firemen's helmets. They sell like hot cakes, and still what are they good for? But you can't tell in advance whether some things will sell or not, like an old family album for instance. Not your own folks, you understand, but pictures of folks you don't know and never heard of. Who wants a lot of pictures of strangers when you don't even know who they are?

"One day I picked up an old album just because there wasn't an'thin' else within reach—and bang! The minute I held it up somebody made a one-dollar bid; and I'd hardly had time to draw my breath when in come a one-fifty. It kept hoppin' along like that until it got up to six or seven dollars. By that time I was gettin' worried because I thought the bidders didn't realize what it was, and that they might make a rumpus when they found out.

"The biddin' was already far above the value of the battered old album, and still there was a lively battle going on between two young fellers who were complete strangers to me. When it touched ten dollars I didn't dare let it go any farther and just hammered it down and declared it sold.

"The loser tried to protest, but I ruled that he was too late, and turned my attention to somethin' entirely different. I half expected trouble from the successful bidder when he found out what he had bought; but he was tickled with his bargain, and as soon as he had paid for it he tucked it under his arm and left the hall.

"My helper spied on him as he went out the door and saw him stop in the entry and remove several little old pictures from the back of the album. He pocketed these, threw the album into a trash barrel and went away. The book was immediately rescued by the unsuccessful bidder who ran rapidly through the pages and chucked it back in the trash barrel with a disgruntled snort.

"All this made my helper mighty inquisitive. 'Didn't I see you biddin' on that album?' he asked.

"The fellow glanced at him. 'I bid on it all right, but the other fellow got it.'

" 'But why did you throw it away?'

" 'Because that guy took out what I wanted. Now it's worthless.'

" 'You mean those little pi'tures?'

" 'I certainly do.'

" 'Was they relatives of yours?'

" 'Relatives my uncle!' the fellow muttered. 'Those pictures had rare and valuable revenue stamps on the back of 'em.'

" 'But how do you know that?'

" 'Because I examined that book before the sale. But so'd the other guy; I saw him. Nowadays smart stamp collectors are on the lookout for all old family albums. Why, I know a fellow who found a hundred dollars worth of stamps in a cracked-up old album that cost him only half a dollar.' "

The auctioneer rubbed his hands together. "Now do you see why I said you can't always tell why people bid? I know what I'm talkin' about for I've seen some mighty peculiar things. You take an old broken tombstone, for instance. We've got little old cemeteries around here well over two hundred years old, and gravestones don't last forever, you know. Sometimes the frost makes 'em brittle, or they got coated with ice, and then a stiff wind comes along and snaps 'em right off. Well, you don't want the gravestones of your ancestors layin' around on the ground for people to walk on, so naturally you take 'em home.

"There's hardly a dooryard in this neighborhood that hasn't got a busted gravestone layin' around somewhere. They're smooth, you know, carved on only one side, and they make a mighty good well stone, or even a hearthstone. All the old-time auctioneers used to sell 'em, and a friend of mine is using one for a doorstep right now, not a mile away from here. I'll give

you the address and you can go over and see it. I don't recollect
the name or the date on it, but I can't forget that epitaph.

Here lies my wife
What better can she do
For her repose
And mine, too?

"That may sound funny to you. It does to me. But if his
wife is waitin' for him 'Beyond the River' he may find that she
still can't take a joke. She never could when she was alive.

"Well, I suppose you want to ask me about the most unfor-
gettable day in my forty-odd years of auctioneerin', and I can
tell you right off the reel that it was the 22nd day of June, 1935,
when I sold seven schoolhouses in a single day between sunup
and sundown. The fact is that I wasn't no schoolhouse specialist.
I never had sold one before that day, and I've never sold another
since, and never expect to. You see there was a new law passed
allowin' the consolidatin' of all the little one-room district
schools in the township into one big central schoolhouse with
all the grades and everythin' in one enormous building.

"There'd be no more hikin' a mile or two on the way to school
through storm and snow and zero weather, and like as not havin'
to build a fire in the stove for the teacher after you got there.
Then there was water to fetch from the nearest well, sometimes
a quarter of a mile away with the old oaken bucket covered with
ice. The only plumbin' was in the back yard hid behind a
highboard fence, and there was no playground except what we
made for ourselves among the thistles and the poison ivy.

"One room and one teacher, and sometimes forty pupils of
all ages from six to sixteen. But no more of that. Now the big
yellow buses would call for and deliver the children to a model
school with a separate room and teacher for every grade, a
drinkin' fountain instead of a pail and dipper, white plumbin'

in the basement where it would be warm in winter and cool in summer, not a wood-box or a coal scuttle in sight, a big assembly room, and a good basketball team. It's almost like goin' to college. The only drawback was that a boy couldn't take his dog to school with him any more.

"The new buildin' wasn't entirely ready when the district schools closed in June for the summer vacation. But it was near enough done so they knew it would be ready for the openin' of the fall term; and the members of the school board decided to sell the old schoolhouses as soon as school let out so as to have a little money on hand for emergencies that might come up.

"And right then was the time when they called me in as auctioneer. They sorta had a habit of callin' me in for this, that, and the other thing. I had served a considerable term as tax collector; I'd been senior warden and sexton of my church for a good many years; I'd been foreman of the jury, and once I represented the town as a member of the lower house in Hartford. A few of my other jobs was tax assessor, fire warden, member of the school board, and did I say tree warden? I guess no other auctioneer was even thought of.

"I accepted, of course, and advertised the auction, and then I sat down and figured out the most convenient road route so I wouldn't double on my tracks too much. And so a little before ten o'clock on that famous day I come drivin' up in my old Ford and stopped before the schoolhouse on the corner of Hammertown and Great Ring roads. There wasn't a big crowd, but it wasn't much of a schoolhouse. I had set my heart on gettin' about $500, but all I could squeeze out of 'em was $450. That included the buildin' and the lot. When I drove away a couple of carloads of folks come followin' after me.

"The next two schoolhouses was little fellers, both on rented ground which meant that the buyer would have to tear 'em down or take 'em away. I figured they would bring about $50 apiece for two of the local churches had showed an interest in 'em to use as an addition to the church clubhouse or kitchen. I was lookin' for a mite of a contest because these two churches wasn't any too fond of each other. There was quite a crowd at the first one and a lot of cars parked around—but there was no competition at all. The East Village school went to the Liberal Christian Church for a single bid of $25. I tried my best to get the Apostolic Brothers to bid against them, but they never made a peep. So I had to let it go.

"I fussed around there for a while gettin' the down payment and writin' out a receipt and I asked one of the Apostolic boys why they didn't bid, and he laughed and said that the price was too high. When I moved on a lot of cars come followin' along. This time I was really lookin' for a hassel. I was all set for some lively bidding, but there was no competition at all. Just a single bid—and it was all over. Only this time it was the Apostolic Brothers who did the biddin' and they got their schoolhouse for $50. Things began to look a little queer to me. Here I had figured to get $100 for the two, and all I got was $75. I had brought my lunch with me, and while I was sittin' in my car eatin', one of the school board members come along and stopped to pass the time of day. Finally he said to me in a guarded tone, 'What's goin' on around here?'

" 'Well,' I said with a smile, 'We're havin' an auction—I guess.'

" 'You better guess again,' he muttered. "It looks more like collusion.'

"I was startled. 'What do you mean by that?' I demanded.

" 'It's the Old Army Game,' he said. 'If you'll agree not to bid on my schoolhouse, I won't bid on yours. See what I mean?'

" 'No collusion about it,' I argued. 'Everybody in town knows that each church wanted to get the nearest schoolhouse. Neither church has got any too much money, so I guess folks just let 'em bid in the property for a reasonable price. I'd call it charity, not collusion.'

" 'Is that the way you feel about the deals put over by the

notorious "Forty Thieves" of the auction ring?' he demanded.

" 'Not at all,' I replied indignantly. 'Those fellows are a lot of crooks. They're out to cheat people.'

" 'But these schoolhouses belong to the town. So you think it's all right to cheat the town, do you?' he asked scornfully.

" 'I can't make people bid if they don't want to,' I said. 'But the town could have bid up the two schoolhouses as high as they wanted to. You were right here—a member of the school board—why didn't *you* do it yourself?'

"He backed down in a hurry. 'Well, it really wasn't my place,' he said. 'You see, I had no authority. Guess after all there's no harm done. Where do you go from here?'

"I allowed I was goin' to Elm Street school, and he went on his way. Curiously enough no two of these schoolhouses was alike. They was never the same size or shape. You'd reckonize 'em as schoolhouses but the windows would be scattered around on 'em in almost any old place; the door was never where you expected it to be. And the Elm Street school was the only one in town that had hitchin' posts. Just why they was there I never could figure; they never was used, and never had been used as far as I can recollect. There was a good well on the lot, but the building was small and was located on an unimproved road. Still it was worth the hunderd and four dollars it brought.

"More papers to sign, and then the crowd was off for Purdy Hill where the Cutler Farm schoolhouse was located. By this time the parade had turned into a reg'lar carnival; musta been a dozen cars. People was callin' back and forth from one car to another, and occasionally they would exchange passengers just for fun and variety—fellers and girls. Guess I was the only serious-minded person in the crowd, and I was busy figgerin' how I could get the best price for the next school.

"The Cutler Farm school was the only one with a front porch, though it was smaller than some of the others; and yet there was a time when that schoolroom had accommodated fifty-four scholars with a single teacher who taught all eight grades, and taught them pretty good for a salary of $450 a year. The house went for only $50—lot not included.

"Lower Stepney schoolhouse come next with even more cars joinin' the procession. This was a real attractive building with the advantage of bein' on a numbered road, and the disadvantage of bein' on three roads, for it was on a lot in the middle of the junction point. Another important sellin' point was a good artesian well. It didn't flow, but it come close to the surface of the ground. Bidders were all around the place when I pounded for order. We started with a bid of five hunderd and had half a dozen different bidders before we reached a thousand. And there it hung with an old Irish fellow holdin' the bid. It was a nice place and I didn't especially want him to get it, for he always kept pigs around, and this was too nice a place for pigs —on the best street in town. So I give a kind of a nod to one of the other bidders, and he kinda caught on and raised the bid ten dollars and quick as a wink I slammed down my hammer and hollered *Sold!* The old Mick tried make a protest, but he was too late.

"The sale come along soon after the repeal of the Prohibition Amendment when the entire country was pretty upset, especially the dyed-in-the-wool drys. They took it pretty hard, and when the title to this property come to be passed it was found that a little joker has been slipped into the deed providing that liquor should never be sold on the premises "so long as the grass grows green and water flows in the brook."

"It was that part about the grass that caught the buyer's eye, but he was a genial easygoin' feller and was inclined to let the thing go; but his wife would have none of it. She was by no means a soppin'-wet, nor was she a hidebound dry; but the property had been bought without any restrictions and she insisted that the deed must be free and clear in every way.

"Caught in the act, the scrivener, who was a rabid dry, somewhat sheepishly give in, but when the new deed was drawn it was found to be on an ordinary quitclaim form which guaranteed nothin'. And once more it was the buyer's wife who got her back up and insisted on a warranty deed.

"This little trick brought some pretty sharp language on the part of the town clerk, and finally the warranty deed came through. At the time I was sellin' this property I hadn't the least idear that all these complications were in the cards, and once the deal was closed and the down payment made I turned all my attention to the Birdseye Plains schoolhouse in Upper Stepney.

"This Birdseye school was the gem of our educational efforts. Like all the rest of 'em it was without so much as a suspicion of indoor plumbin', but the buildin' had two large rooms and was located fairly well off the road on a nice lot of about four acres, and it had a good well into the bargain. But the truth is that I was not thinkin' about these things; instead my mind was turning back to the days of my childhood, for this was the first school I ever went to.

"As I pulled out of Route 25 and come to a stop in the schoolyard I could see with half an eye that the biggest crowd of the day was already waitin' there, and a glance down the road told me that a lot of overloaded jalopies was comin' along behind me and I felt pretty sure that little old Birdseye was goin' out in a blaze of glory.

"The reason why the whole neighborhood should go sentimental over the passin' of the little old red schoolhouse is not for me to say. It was more like a funeral than a picnic, and I noticed that some of the former pupils put in a little bid just for old time's sake, though they had no intention of buyin'. Of course these were cautious bids made early enough so there was no possible chance of havin' the property struck down to them. It was like joinin' in the Lord's Prayer in church where you are not so much speakin' to the Lord as mumblin' for the benefit of your neighbor in the next pew.

"After this sentimental biddin' was over the sale settled down to a duel between a couple of determined bidders until the property was finally knocked down to a woman who wanted the buildin' for remodelin' into a house. And with the old-fashioned desks still bolted to the floors, the erasers heavy with chalk dust on the base of the blackboard, the empty water pail and dipper perched on the shelf in the corner, the Round Oak stove a little rusty but standin' sturdylike on its battered zinc floor mat, my trusty hammer come down on her bid of $2,650—and the district school of Birdseye Plains was no more.

"As I laid down my hammer and mopped my brow I says in a voice that didn't sound much like a bellowin' auctioneer, 'Well, I guess this school's goin' to have a long vacation.' And sure enough it has.

"Now I suppose you'll want to ask me what was the most thrillin' and excitin' day in my auction career, and I can tell you right out of hand what it was. It was once when I was havin' a big dispersal auction up on the Poverty Hollow road. George Hobbs had been workin' a farm up there practically all his life, but his family had grown up and got married, and had gone off to the city to live. For a while him and his wife had lived there together with a couple of hired men doin' most of the farm work, and then she up and died—as a feller's wife will do. That left George there all alone except for the hired help.

"George stuck it out for a while with a disagreeable housekeeper who had a couple of unruly kids, and then he decided to sell out and go to Los Angeles and spend the rest of his borrowed time with his oldest son who was a real estate man, like everybody else in Los Angeles.

"It was to be a full dispersal, horses, cows, hogs, sheep, in fact everythin' includin' household furniture and even a cellar full of canned goods and a couple of barrels of cider. George went in for blooded stock and had one Black Angus bull worth around $2,500. Angus, as they called him would have brought a lot more money only he had a bad disposition and reputation as a fence-crasher. He would go through an ordinary fence like it was an open gate. If there was a cow in heat within a half a mile you couldn't stop him—he'd get there somehow. At least that's the way George used to tell it. He insisted that bull could get loose any time he wanted to, and they used to say that when he did break out the entire neighborhood would climb a tree, and that even inside the house the womenfolks would go up in the attic and and lock the door behind 'em just to be on the safe side. Well, to get on with my story, George had a nice little herd of about a dozen yearlin' heifers that he kept on another farm, but he brought 'em over to be sold at the auction and put 'em on display in a field next to the back lawn where the auction was to be held.

"These little fellers was black as a coalminer's fingernails, and not at all shy, and even with a crowd of folks standin' along the fence lookin' an' lookin' at 'em they just nibbled quietly at the grass in the meadow and paid no attention to the visitors. I was just finishin' off the last of the household articles which had been brought outside and stacked in front of the big hay barn so everybody could see 'em, when I heard from somewhere in the maze of buildins behind me a muffled bellow that I recognized as the voice of the cooped-up Angus. And one of those yearlins a little more pert and sassy than the rest must also have heard it, for she stretched out her little black neck and answered it with all the yearnin' sweetness of the springtime. Well, sir, just as if it had been a signal, all the other little heifers began bawlin' and bellowin' with joy unconfined, though they couldn't all of 'em have known much about the birds and the butterflies.

"This musical hubbub hadn't been goin' on for more than a

few seconds when the barn door behind me burst open and a terrified stranger come rushin' out closely pursued by the bull with lowered head and flyin' heels, its nostrils dilated and snortin' with every breath.

"Whether it was the man or the bull that hit my foldin' podium I couldn't say, but I went topplin' some four feet to the ground—gettin' a good jolt and sprainin' my thumb. I scrambled to my feet just in time to see the bull hook one of those red foldin' chairs with a horn and throw it clear up into an apple tree.

"How he ever happened to pick an empty chair I wouldn't know, for there was more than a hundred occupied ones right within reach. That is, they was occupied when he come out that door, but they was all of 'em empty within a couple of split seconds and most of 'em knocked over by the occupants who was tryin' to skate across the top of 'em like Eliza crossin' the ice to get on the other side of the yard where the bull couldn't get at them.

"But they needn't have been worried about the bull—he was not interested in 'em. In fact, he was not interested in the man he was supposed to be chasin'; he might even have been grateful to the inquisitive snooper for openin' the inner door of his prison to peer inside and rushin' away without closin' it when he got a glimpse of the Angus.

In spite of all the cries, the screamin', and the confusion, the bull went straight to those heifers, takin' a section of the fence with him. But his sudden appearance frightened the little heifers. His bellowin' silenced them. And when he begun to paw the ground they turned tail and went frolickin' off across the field, head and tail up, and their heels kickin' high. Completely baffled, the big chunky Black Angus stood among the fragments of the fence, his forefeet wide apart, his neck stretched straight out, his tail lashin' back and forth, while

George Hobbs walked slowly up to him and snapped the leading pole to the ring in his nose.

"People were still dustin' off their clothes and huntin' for their hats among the overturned chairs when George led Angus up in front of the crowd where he stood as docile as an old family ox.

" 'I hope nobody was seriously hurt,' said George.

"Some barked shins and a few torn stockins were reported, but my thumb seemed to be the most serious casualty.

" 'All right,' said George. 'Now that we've got him out here we may as well sell him.'

" 'Well we did, and he brought an even $2,750, which was a pretty nice endin' for my most excitin' day as an auctioneer, for I was workin' on a straight 10 per cent commission."

CHAPTER ELEVEN

STAMP AUCTIONEERING

THE AUCTIONEERING OF STAMPS IS AS MUCH OF AN ART AS THE selling of jewelry, old and rare books, or paintings by the inspired Old Masters, for the stamp business is so full of ins and outs that the ordinary shouting auctioneer who feels that he must hold every object in his hands and show how it works in order to sell it, would feel very much out of place in attempting to auction off a postage stamp from a number or a photographic illustration in a catalogue.

The successful stamp auctioneer is no ballyhoo man, no mere mouthpiece who keeps up a chant or chatter to confuse his bidders and hold their attention. Nor does he strut about waving his hands and gesticulating. He is much more likely to sit at ease in a chair on the rostrum with a table in front of him and a paperweight in his hand instead of the old-fashioned hammer. He is keenly alert to see where his bids are coming from, and when made he repeats them so that there may be no misunderstanding.

Some of the large galleries have a battery of four or five auctioneers, most of them specialists, one on paintings, another on old and rare books, another on antiques, and in all probability a man well informed on the subject of philately in these days when single stamps run up into the thousands, and collections into the millions. And since all in the audience will have had an opportunity for a previous examination of all the philatelic offerings, no extended explanations on the part of the auctioneer are required, and sales are made entirely by catalogue number.

Where the stamp auctions cash in is on selling the big collections, especially the kind with a chain reaction which goes on and on through a series of separate auctions running to a dozen and a half or even more before the entire collection has been disposed of.

Only recently Mr. H. R. Harmer, the well-known New York stamp auctioneer, sold a used block of eight Savoy Cross stamps issued at Naples, Italy, in 1860 for $19,000. And this might not have thrilled him too much, for later that same day he auctioned off a collection of stamps from the Old Italian States for $263,000. This occurred at the seventh in a series of sixteen auctions, each continuing from three days to a week as part of a plan for the disposition of what is said to be the most notable stamp collection in the world, that of the late Albert H. Caspary, formerly a New York stock broker. It might be added that the receipts for the auctions already held have amounted to $2,537,422. And it is expected that by the end of 1958 the total amount realized by the sale of the entire Caspary collection may go over three million.

The reason for the placing of this magnificent collection on the market is quite simply that Mr. Caspary preferred that his philatelic holdings should be dispersed among a large number of private collectors rather than have them permanently laid away in one of the great public museums; and he so provided in his will with instructions that the proceeds of the sale should be distributed to various charities.

According to a whim of fate, the most costly and desirable stamps are by no means the most beautiful or the most historically important. Freaks and scarcity are the two qualities most sought after by the collectors, and accordingly bring the auc-

tioneers some of their largest commissions. With stamps as with
books, scarcity is their most valuable ingredient from the collector's viewpoint. Some of the most costly books in the world
are often almost unreadable; and many of the rarest of stamps
would not be accepted at any post office to carry the mail
although some of them are worth thousands of dollars to collectors, and many of them are worth more canceled than new.

The most famous and probably the most valuable stamp in
the world today is the British Guiana 1-cent magenta. It is the
only one of its kind, and is the one definitive British colonial
rarity not to be found in the British royal collection. It is
priced in *Scott's Standard Postage Stamp Catalogue* at $50,000,
but its owner, whose identity is carefully hidden, is said to have
received offers of twice that amount for it. One can't help
wondering why he keeps it, for it adds nothing to his fame or
well-being, and he might find some of that money useful. The
fable is that only the one stamp was made so that an officer's
wife on a lonely army post could impress a visitor.

Sometimes I wonder how an auctioneer keeps a straight face
when he stands before an audience and sells for thousands of
dollars a scrap of paper that is worth intrinsically nothing. How
can he refrain from smiling when he sees several otherwise
normal persons panting and trembling with excitement as they
bid for a small bluish envelope bearing the notation 10 *cents*?
Why does anybody want it? Simply because it is the only one
known to have gone through the mail in 1845 from Baltimore to
Annapolis. It is signed by James M. Buchanan who was at the
time Postmaster of Baltimore. The word PAID is twice hand-
stamped on it, and there is a return address in red which reads,
"Barnum's City Hotel, Monument Square, Baltimore."

This unique specimen was sold at auction by H. R. Harmer,
Inc., for $14,000; and on the same day Mr. Harmer also sold
at auction 153 covers made and autographed by other early
postmasters for $225,340.

If I had known about this a few years ago I could have made myself quite a little nest egg, for I have thrown away dozens of just such covers found in the attic of my old home in upstate New York when I was a boy. I even used some of them as wrappers for cornsilk cigarettes and actually smoked them though they were neither king-size nor filtered and I must admit that I did not care much for the taste.

Before the days of the stamp auctions it was the dealer who called the tune and named the market price for all collectible postage stamps. He could mark the price up or down according to his whim. His control of quotations was not unlike the market "pools" which regulated Wall Street prices in the old days before Wall Street itself was regulated. However, in the field of philately the public auctions have changed the picture radically, for although they are largely conducted by firms composed of dealers, the bidding process in itself has given the collectors the whip hand. They can by their bidding drive the prices upward when an offering is scarce and downward when it shows signs of becoming plentiful.

Hundreds of single stamps are being held today at $1,000, but very few at $20,000. A Lockport, N. Y., postmaster provisional, 5-cent red and black on buff, is now quoted at $12,000, probably not far from the valuation of the entire post office building from which it was issued. Its principal value, of course, is its rarity, for there is only one and it is dated 1846. There is nothing pictorial about it, simply one oval inside another and the words:

LOCKPORT

PAID

$5

N. Y.

The first commemorative postage stamp in the United States was in celebration of the one hundredth anniversary of American Independence in 1876 known as the Centennial Exhibition. Strictly speaking it was not a stamp at all, but a stamped envelope. New South Wales may have borrowed the idea from us, for it was not long afterward when she came out with a set of ten stamps to celebrate her own centenary as a colony of the British Crown. These stamps were dispersed over a period of two years. Hong Kong was the next to follow suit when she brought out a single stamp to commemorate her first half-century under the British flag.

However, we were beaten on the commemoration of the four hundredth anniversary of the discovery of America by Columbus, for Argentina, Honduras, and Paraguay came out with Columbian stamps appropriate to the occasion in 1892, whereas our own Columbian stamp missed the boat, because of mechanical difficulties and probably faulty memories, and our Columbian commemoratives did not reach our post-office counters until January, 1893. It was an almost, but a miss is as good as a mile. However, our Columbian series of sixteen stamps starting at one cent and going to five dollars met with instant public favor, became immediate best sellers and achieved a sale of more than two billion copies in fifteen months.

Our Columbian half-dollar was also a great success and jingled as a lucky piece in the pants pockets of America for many years. Indeed, I discovered one a few days ago lying tarnished in a bureau drawer in our attic—and I didn't spend it, just as I haven't spent it every time I've come across it in the fifty-four years since it came from the mint.

There are those who dispute that the Columbian stamp was our initial commemorative, claiming that honor for the black 15-cent stamp issued on June 17, 1866, bearing the likeness of Abraham Lincoln. Coming as it did a year after his death it was undoubtedly commemorative, but was made necessary at this time because of an increase in the fee charged on registered mail.

Mauritz Hallgren in his book *All About Stamps* tells of the days when the philatelic enthusiasts had their hangout on Nassau Street just as the Stock Market clings to Wall Street. The stamp market had its bid and asked prices, and quotations which were as regularly reported as the movements of the bulls and the bears. He speaks of its tipsters, dope sheets, market analysts, short sales, and attempted corners. This may all be so, for certainly the stamp speculators play the market today with great acumen and shrewdness. They take their winnings with delight and their losses with the usual amount of growling, but on the whole they are probably no better guessers than the postal authorities who pick the commemoratives or the men at the race tracks who select the probable winners.

But no more than a glance is needed at the advertising pages of the New York papers to show that the philatelic market with its auctioneers, dealers, traders and hangers-on has followed the popular trend toward uptown and is now scattered about the fashionable Forties and Fifties contiguous to the big-time auction galleries where the moneyed collectors and speculators prefer to carry on their buying and selling and playing their hunches.

The idea of cornering the market in postage stamps seems at a first glance about as impossible as cornering hot air in the halls of Congress. But it has been done at least once, and that was with the harmless little 1-cent green of the 1922 series. This was an imperforate edition specially prepared for use in the vending machines and printed in long rolls instead of the customary small sheets of 100 stamps each perforated on all four sides. For some seven years after publication these particular rolls were on sale to the public at face value by the government Philatelic Agency, and not until 1929 when the entire stock of the government had been exhausted did the fact come to light that a few far-sighted speculators had been quietly buying and now controlled the remaining supply of the issue.

The owners of these stamps played the game very cautiously;

they did nothing to arouse the suspicions of the government, but went on selling the stamps to users at a slight advance in price until the end of the year by which time they had gone up about six cents a copy. Then suddenly the owners put on the screws and jumped the price to one dollar and in some cases even more. At this price the investors unloaded, selling at three or four hundred dollars a sheet stamps that had cost them only four dollars at the government price. It was no such operation as a corner in wheat or sugar would have been, but it was a neat little transaction.

Selling stamps at public auction was begun as an experiment in 1870 when it was tried in New York without much success by a stouthearted philatelist named J. Walter Scott. The highest bid for a single stamp was eleven dollars and the total receipts for the sale came to only $500; and a curious circumstance was that the eleven-dollar stamp was later quoted at $3,000. The general impression was that the auctioneering of stamps would never amount to much.

But Scott was a persistent fellow and two years later he tried again, this time in Britain. His auction was held at Sotheby's with such resounding success that the stamp auction has since become the accepted method of selling both separate items and the enormous collections put together by prince and potentate or men of great wealth who have spent a lifetime in amassing rare and costly stamps as a hobby.

While there is today a constant trading going on between individual collectors by means of philatelic clubs, and classified advertising, this is puny in amount compared with the philatelic material handled by the huge public auctions which are continually in operation in all parts of the civilized world. Indeed, the stamp business has become so immense and so complicated that no well-informed collector who acquires a really valuable item even dreams of handling it for himself any more than a wise investor would think of launching a bond issue or buying a railroad without the services of a bank or brokerage firm.

Some of the large stamp establishments buy and sell a general line of all kinds of philatelic material while others specialize in commemoratives, airmails, covers, or the stamps of some particular country or continent, all of them hoping to come across a real rarity someday and make a killing. These finds are not impossible. One of the most famous in our own country was the twenty-four-cent airmail stamp with the plane turned upside down. This was sold to a broker's clerk who handled stamps on the side. He bought the entire sheet of 100 for which he paid the man at the window $24. He had no difficulty in selling the unbroken sheet to speculators who quickly sold it by telephone, sight unseen, to Col. E. H. R. Green, a famous collector and the son of Hetty, for $20,000. Not a bad deal, for the time came when the single stamps from that sheet sold as high as $4,100.

The first known stamp show was reputedly held in Brussels in 1852. There seems to have been only one exhibitor, a Belgian geographer named Phillippe Vandermaalen. He had very few stamps to show at the time and very little interest was taken in the affair. Nothing more was heard about a stamp exhibition for a quarter of a century when the next attempt was made, this time at Antwerp. It must have been a modest show, for although it was mentioned in the press no details were given. Next in order came an exhibition in America in 1889. Little is known about the show or the auspices under which it was given; however, it must have been a macabre occasion for it was held—of all places—at the Eden Musée. Anybody who has ever visited this home of the waxworks cannot fail to recall that the scenes depicted were almost exclusively those of bloodshed and horror. Just where stamps could have been exhibited in such ghoulish surroundings is beyond imagination.

The first mail-order auction I attended was at one of the big international stamp companies in New York City. I saw a tiny advertisement in the Sunday paper of a three-day auction which

was scheduled for the latter part of July and wrote for a catalogue, receiving by return mail a 56-page illustrated booklet
describing 1059 lots of stamps which were going under the
hammer, with three exhibition days scheduled during the week
prior to the auction.

Enclosed with the catalogue was a folding envelope to be
used as a "Bid Form." The bidding is really a rather simple
matter. The bidder enters his name and address on the form and
indicates the particular session of the auction at which he desires
to bid. On the face of the ballot are 100 blank spaces in which
to specify the number of the lot and the highest price at which
he desires to bid on it. There is a printed provision on the blank
that all lots will be sold to the bidder below these limits if the
auction permits.

The first session, which was to be held July 22, was to include
lots numbered 1 to 399 inclusive; the second session, scheduled
for July 23, would include lots numbered 400 to 747; and the
third session, scheduled for July 24, would begin with lot
numbered 748 and end with 1059 for the conclusion of the sale.

A catalogue description was precise. It indicated the color of
the stamp, the denomination, the date of issue, and the condition
which was specified as: superb, very fine, fine, very good, good,
fair, and poor. The importance of gum on a stamp was fully
dealt with: "Part o.g.," meaning that stamp is unused with part
of original gum; "o.g." means that stamp is unused with original
gum slightly disturbed, usually because of a previous hinge.
"Mint" means unused with original gum in post office state but
mounted with a peelable hinge, and "n.h." means never hinged,
unused with original gum in post office state and unmounted.

Even the condition of the perforations is specified, for any
government imperfection in the manufacture of a stamp adds
greatly to its value.

And for each item in the catalogue, an estimated value is given
in the final column as a guide to the bidder. The letter A fol-

lowed by a plus sign denotes an increase in the value of the catalogue price for one or more reasons. For collections or large lots, "Est. Cash Val." means estimated cash value, and is used for a group of items which are not individually priced. A plus sign after the price of a mint sheet indicates that it has been catalogued as single copies.

The auction room high up in a building not far from Rockefeller Center was about half filled when I entered. It was the usual setup of rows of folding chairs arranged like an amphitheater, with a rostrum so high in elevation that a standing man's head would just clear the ceiling. Beside the towering rostrum was a fairly long table on floor level at which sat a stunning girl surrounded by stamp albums. She handed me a catalogue and smiled prettily as she invited me to take a seat, which I did well back in the room from which I could see everything that was going on.

As two o'clock approached the place quickly filled, and in looking around I discovered that the audience was made up entirely of men, most of them balding and not one of them under fifty.

At the stroke of two the auctioneer entered from an adjoining office and ascended the rostrum. He couldn't have been over forty, and he was all business. He sat down, opened a catalogue, and spread it before him on the table. "We are starting today with lot 400," he announced. "Postage and Air Post imprint. Blocks of four." He raised his eyes from the catalogue and glanced quickly around the room. "Do I hear an offer?" There was no answer. "I have a mail order for fourteen dollars. Any more from anybody?" Another silence. "Sold at fourteen."

Then came a few small sales and one or two mail bids, and after that a collection of stamps from Afghanistan. The catalogue gave an Est. Cash Val. of $25, but some rapid-fire bidding from the audience ran the price up to $42. In another case a mail-order bid for $5 purchased a 1928 Air Post with a catalogue

listing of $28, and shortly afterward another mail bid won a
$109 item for $55.

As fast as the lots were called the girl with the stamp books
would hold up a portfolio and exhibit the stamp or block so the
bidders could check what they were bidding on. There was
quite a stir throughout the room when an $85 bid won a col-
lection with a catalogue value of $600. There were no really
big headliners that day, the most costly single stamp sold at
the auction being an 1861 regular issue 3-cent pink, o.g., fresh,
fine, with A.P.S. certificate, priced at $300. However, several of
the catalogue pages totaled $2,000 or more, and fully a third
of the successful bids were those which had been received by
mail.

The catalogue announced that during the year the firm had
sold by auction from a noted private collection stamps totaling
more than a million and a half, and during the same time the
run-of-the-mill rostrum sales had exceeded eight hundred thousand dollars, with reservations in hand for over a million more.
And this is only one firm out of the seven columns of stamp
dealers listed in the yellow pages of the New York Telephone
Book.

So that little brown five-cent postage stamp with the portrait
of Ben Franklin on the front, and gum on the back, that was
first printed in 1847 by a job printer in New York City, really
started something that is still going great guns and may at some
not too distant future time be found carrying letters to the
moon.

CHAPTER TWELVE

SCHOOL DAYS

WHILE INTERVIEWING AN AUCTIONEER ONE DAY, I HAPPENED TO ask him where he learned the business. He said he was self-taught, but if he had it to do over again he would go to one of the auction schools. He went on to say that the best auctioneer he had ever heard once told him that he had gone to an auction school somewhere in the West though he did not mention the name of the place.

I did not know there was such a school, but I was determined to find out. So I wrote to a number of the big universities in the West, the East, and on the Pacific Coast inquiring about the matter and receiving uniformly negative answers, and was inclined to believe that my auctioneer friend had been misinformed. Then quite unexpectedly I found in the classified columns of one of the big agricultural magazines the following four-line advertisement which was hidden between an invitation to "Become a psychologist or metaphysician," and the advice to "Grow mushrooms in your own cellar":

> AUCTIONEERING. Be an auctioneer.
> Term soon. Earn big money. Write for
> catalogue. Kansas City Auction School.
> Kansas City, Missouri.

I wrote for a catalogue and received a small pamphlet as well as a printed letter from the headmaster of the school congratulating me for wanting to become an auctioneer. "Take it from me," he wrote, "I've been in the business since 1919, and there is no profession more rewarding than that of auctioneer; it's interesting, glamorous, inspiring, and pays exceptionally well."

He added in another paragraph, "Here at Kansas City Auction School we have the know-how, the faculty and facilities in our school to make the kind of auctioneer who earns big money. Don't put off your future another day."

The full training in auctioneering was stated to be a two weeks course crowded full of the "Best knowledge and learning." As a graduate of the school I was promised that I would be awarded a "beautiful diploma" and the title of Colonel. Tuition $100 and no other charges or fees except board and lodging during the fourteen days' term. I had hardly finished reading the pamphlet when the "literature" began to come in urging me to join the term beginning the following Monday. The next day I received a group picture from the school with this caption:

Calling all Would-be COLONELS!
Who want a brighter future—
Better living—joy and happiness
By becoming an EXPERT AUCTIONEER.

The next mailing contained a single page with the heading:

AUCTIONEERS! Be One.

ATTENTION! ALL ASPIRING THE TITLE OF COLONEL
AND WANTING TO BECOME A FULL-FLEDGED
AUCTIONEER

OPPORTUNITY is here again for you! We sincerely hope that for your future success you'll take advantage of the forth-coming term etc., etc.

Auctioneeringly yours,

(The name of the President)

Having found one auctioneering school I soon found a classified ad of another, this one located in Fort Smith, Arkansas. The town is described in the catalogue as nestling in the foothills of the famous Ozark Mountains "and could very aptly be termed the hub of the Midwest."

The largest of the schools I finally succeeded in locating—the Reppert School of Auctioneering, in Decatur, Indiana—outlines a course of twelve phases lasting three full weeks plus a promise to teach each student "To run your business, keep your books, and succeed without capital." In another place the catalogue says in red ink, "Reppert training will put you in the Big-Pay-Class."

It seems that Colonel Reppert who originally organized the school was an important figure in American auctioneering. He had operated his profession in every state of the Union as well as Canada and Mexico. He was the first auctioneer to sell a Duroc hog for over $5,000, and won a world's record when he sold a Poland China hog for $21,000. Later he sold a stallion under the hammer for $47,500; then a Hereford bull for $31,000, and a herd of fifty Herefords at an average price of $5,000 a head. All that happened some time ago, and the Colonel is now gone but not forgotten, and the school is being conducted by a younger generation of Repperts, the headmaster being a licensed physician.

I wrote to the school asking if there was not an alumnus

living within a reasonable distance of my home in Connecticut
to whom I could go for some word-of-mouth information about
the school, and promptly received a letter referring me to a
graduate living less than one hundred miles away. I called on
him one day and found him a most agreeable man in the forties
conducting a successful auction house of his own in a small
Connecticut town. He was ready to talk freely and enthusiastically about the Reppert School of Auctioneering, and I will let
him tell his own story just as he told it to my recorder. This is
it:

"The first day I got there was of course registration, and
getting us assigned to our places in the barracks, or the dormitory, as they called it. Then in addition to being registered we
all had to have our voices recorded on a voice-registering
machine. I was thankful this was not done in public because
they had me make a record of selling something at a mock-
auction in the presence of two of the instructors. I was greener
than grass at the time. I had never made a speech in public, and
had never seen a recording machine before, and of course I had
never even tried to conduct an auction or a mock-auction either
—and when they pointed out a wheelbarrow and told me to
go through the motions of selling it, I didn't even know how
to begin. Of course I knew what a wheelbarrow was. Every
country boy knows that, and I'd used one nearly all my life;
but when I stood up in front of that machine to sell it I couldn't
think of a thing to say about it—not a single selling point. I
finally managed to stammer out, 'Well, there it is—you can see
it for yourself. Who'll give me a dollar to start it?'

"A dollar, mind you! I knew perfectly well that wheelbarrow
was worth sixteen or eighteen dollars, and still I was so panicky
that I tried to start it at a dollar. They could see that I was all
befuddled and they didn't push me very hard and I hadn't gone
very many words when they let me quit. They said they had a
good record of my voice and that was all they wanted.

"There was no teaching that day so the fellows spent their time getting acquainted. But the next day right after breakfast we had about fifteen minutes of good fast calisthenics. We used to have calisthenics every day—it was supposed to be body-building. Most of the teaching was done by lectures while the students took notes that they could study and refer to later on. The most important thing in the auction business is articulation. The audience has got to know what you're talking about or they can't bid; and the first things the instructors teach you is how to talk, and keep right on talking as long as there is anything to sell. An auctioneer without a good strong voice will never make a go of it.

"One of the first things you learn is how to call bids. They have a regular lingo for it, and they use a lot of words they call fillers, and you have to memorize those and get so you can rattle them right off without even trying. After a while, especially when you are on your own you'll find that there are words of your own that you keep using. One of my favorites is 'money bid.' I find myself saying it without hardly knowing it. 'Five dollars money bid' or 'seven and a half money bid.' They tell these things to the class, but if anybody isn't clear about it he can raise his hand and they'll explain. And if a fellow still didn't get it he'd have another chance that night, for there was always an instructor or two who'd be around the auditorium or the barracks every evening. I suppose they came to keep things in order, but they did a lot of teaching, too.

"Sometimes an instructor would line us up in two lines—es-pecially at first—and have us recite these chants in unison. It was for voice training and development, and he'd walk up and down listening to the different voices, and once in a while he'd stop us and make a fellow say it alone while he showed him how to do it. One of the favorite chants was a little short one. It went, 'A quarter—*thirty*-five—*half*-a-dollar—*seventy*-five!'

"He'd beat time with his hands and we'd get a lot of snap

into it. After all, it doesn't mean very much, but it isn't intended to. All they wanted to do was to get out a good full tone. At first some of us would get a little hoarse. But voice was something they were very careful about, and if they thought anybody was straining his voice they'd stop him and not let him chant any more that night. They were strong on deep breathing and talking so that the strain didn't come on the vocal chords. That's what the rigamarole, the chant, does for you; it keeps your voice down in your chest and saves your throat. They used to tell us that an auctioneer without a voice was about as effective as a gun without a bullet.

"After we got so we could use our voices, the next thing the school did was to send out and get a supply of merchandise for us to sell; and after we started selling we no longer spent our evenings practicing chants in the auditorium or the dormitory, for we were holding an auction every night in the week except Sunday. We students had to stand up there and sell things whether we wanted to or not.

"The first time I got up to sell I was probably the way they all say they are—for I had all kinds of butterflies fluttering all over the place. When you look out there and see two or three hundred people looking at you—all you can see is faces, and you don't know a person in the crowd, and you can't remember one of the things that you thought you had learned so well in your classes. The instructor hands you an article to sell, and you hold it up for everybody to see. They look at it but nobody says anything, and you can't think of anything to say. The instructor whispers, 'What am I offered?'

"You catch on and repeat that, but you don't know whether it's your voice or somebody else who is speaking, and a near-sighted person in the back asks, 'What is it?' It's a spatula, but you can't think of the word. The instructor prompts you and tells you to go ahead with it. So you brush aside the butterflies and try again. You hear somebody say 'Twenty-five cents,' but

you have no idea who said it. And yet you pull yourself together.

" 'Twenty-five I hear. Who'll make it thirty-five?' A hand
goes up and now you're on your way. The butterflies disappear
and you make a try for fifty and get it; but there it sticks until
the instructor whispers, 'All right, sell it.'

"I did, and I sold a couple of other things before they called
me off. My only trouble was I didn't know who was doing
the bidding for I couldn't seem to see their hands even if they
did raise them. I guess I must have thought they were butterflies.
That trouble continued for a while, but the time came when I
could see the least little flicker of an eyelid. It wasn't safe for
people to scratch an ear or make any kind of a move, or I'd have
them right in the act before they knew what was going on,
even one old lady who reached up to adjust her specs.

"Of course with so many fellows in the class waiting for their
turn nobody was allowed to sell more than three or four articles,
and a few of the fellows didn't get a chance to sell anything at
all. Two of the fellows who called up lost their nerve at
the last minute and refused to go on at all. But there were other
fellows who were almost glib when they were called up to speak
or do anything in class who made a very poor showing when
they saw that sea of grinning faces out there in front of them.
But the instructors handled them very well; they told them
exactly what to do and what to say and explained to the crowd
that the boys were just learning and asked the people to be
patient with them and make things as easy for them as they
could. The crowd was very decent about it, and eventually the
fellows got along all right.

"But the next step that you come to is a little harder, for
instead of just giving you an article to sell, they send you out on
the rostrum to make the opening speech and get the auction
started. Let me explain that we had been taught about that in
class and were expected to get up and tell what kind of an

auction it was, whether it was an estate, or folks moving away, or somebody going out of business, or whatever the facts might be. Then, too, we were supposed to explain the terms, how much had to be cash, and when the purchases had to be removed. Then at the end of the speech we were instructed to pick up some article and begin the selling.

"We had been told to start with something small and then work up to something larger. The first fellow up started with a little box containing two spools of thread, and when he made a sale for ten cents everybody laughed and applauded. Another fellow started with a thimble. People laughed, but that didn't bother him any and he went ahead and made up quite a story about the thimble. He said it was made of solid silver plated with gold, and he sold it for a dollar. But after the show he had to go to the woman who had bought it and get it back again when the instructor explained to him that it was made of brass.

"One or two of the boys started by telling a funny story, and and another started by saying that it was a benefit auction. The instructor who was in charge was just on the verge of getting up and saying that it wasn't so when the speaker pulled the string on him and explained that he was calling it a benefit auction because the practice would be of great benefit to the students after they had graduated and gone into business for themselves. But most of the openings consisted of a brief description of the article to be sold and ended with the question, 'What am I offered to get the auction started?'

"You asked me if it was easy to get acquainted when I went there. Well, it was for me and I think it was for most of the fellows. We had something in common—we were all there for the same purpose. All in the same boat. We got to swapping names right off and telling where we had come from, and by lights-out that first night we were all pretty well acquainted. After our bunks were allotted and we knew our places it was a good deal like going into the army. There you were and there you were going to stay for a while, and it wasn't long before we began to feel like one big family.

"Bellmount Park where the auditorium and dormitory are located is about two miles from the center of Decatur and not more than half the fellows there had cars, but I never started to walk from one to the other that somebody didn't pick me up for a ride. I never saw anyone get much farther than the end of the lane before catching a ride. You never even had to wave your thumb. They would drive up beside you and stop for you to get aboard. Remember we were there for only three weeks and it was all work and no play. If there was an auction we'd go there; if not, we'd get together in the auditorium or the barracks where we'd just naturally form into little groups of eight or ten where we would be discussing the lessons and instructions we had received that day. If you felt like argufying you'd join a talking group; but if you wanted a little choir practice or felt like exercising your voice you would get into one of the chanting groups. But even in a talking group you never could be sure that somebody wouldn't start a chant—and if they did, everybody would join in just for the fun of it.

"It was a pretty noisy place, but most of the time we were so busy we didn't pay much attention to the racket going on around us—but if I ever did stop and listen it made me think of the monkey house at the zoo. I don't mean anything bad by that—I just mean that all talking animals are a good deal alike—they enjoy hearing the sound of their own voice.

"The end of the third week was commencement time. We had a big dinner for the whole graduating class with speeches and all that, and then they called us up and gave us our diplomas. I told you how when we first came everybody had to make a record of his voice on a recording machine. Well, one of the last things we did was to line up and make the other side of the record so we can all see how much of a change there is, how much improvement everybody has made—if any. I've got my record around here somewhere yet. But remember this, it was private the first time, but not the second, for every person in that school was there, and most of them were a little nervous.

"You remember that first time they made me go through the motions of selling a wheelbarrow, and I couldn't think of anything to say about it? Well, this time all they gave me to sell was a hoe, and I told them plenty about it. I even worked in a chant, the one about 'Quarter-*thirty*-five—*half*-a-dollar—*seventy*-five.' It went over all right. The fellows got a good laugh out of it, and I was pretty well satisfied myself when I went into the barracks with my diploma tied up in a blue ribbon and put it into my suitcase.

"I suppose you think we ought to have had a commencement ball. But how could we—there never were any ladies around? There was never any kind of entertainment. It was all business every minute of the day familiarizing ourselves with the best methods of selling real estate, household goods, registered livestock, merchandise, antiques such as they were, and everything that can be converted into cash. Then there was physical culture every day to keep us physically and mentally fit and there was a lot to be done with voice development. We had to make a study of real estate, how to develop it and sell it, and there was actual judging of livestock to do on the hoof as well as defining and reading pedigrees. Another thing we went into thoroughly was advertising and salesmanship including a lecture on how to go after auctioneering business—and get it; but all through that three weeks course there was a constant fight against stage fright. Perhaps we got more of that than anything else, unless it was the idea that the bigger the crowd the better the chances of making a sale.

"With all this going on how do you suppose we had any time for fun or entertainment? To tell you the honest truth, we didn't."

CHAPTER THIRTEEN

AUCTIONS AMONG THE STARS

IN THE MOVIE COLONY AT HOLLYWOOD A LIVELY AUCTION IS considered almost as good a source of publicity as a fairly indecent scandal. Anything to get one's name and perhaps a picture into the papers. This is particularly true among those who are comparatively unknown or the "bit actors" who will do almost anything for publicity. Bidding at an auction can become sensational if properly rehearsed in advance. And giving an auction for one charity or another is something that the well-known stars are not averse to doing, and doing in a very dignified and gracious manner.

I have before me some clippings from a "White Elephant Sale" given by Loretta Young a while back for the benefit of St. Anne's Maternity Hospital for Unmarried Mothers. A worthy charity if I ever heard of one. There is something about unmarried mothers which has a strong appeal in Hollywood and the newspaper accounts of that sale fairly sparkled with the names of stars and starlets.

Actor Ray Milland was reported as having bought six Brazilian silver spoons; and Hedy Lamarr was credited with bidding in a single brass candlestick. Mary Pickford was mentioned as having bought an old-time whale-oil lamp converted to electricity, and Frank Sinatra received a brief mention for

buying a gold pen and pencil set. But it was Howard Hughes
who spread himself by purchasing a two-inch gold heart, arrow-
pierced and dripping a blood-red ruby. This I would have
liked to see; or Clark Gable walking out of the auction room
carrying in his arms a century-old chest containing three drawers, followed by tall Gary Cooper toting a pair of china dogs
dating back to 1770. And Joan Bennett must have looked very
fetching carrying home a lace Dresden doll on a china couch.

Hollywood likes class at its auctions, and in announcing a
sale at a Bel-Air home where furniture and paintings were to
be sold, the following notice was given:

> "Only chauffeur-driven cars will be
> allowed on the property; bidders and
> spectators will be conveyed by bus
> from Bel-Air's east gate."

Again the beautiful Hedy Lamarr gets into print when she
places with an auctioneer for disposal the surplus rings from her
first three marriages which were no longer operative. This
would have been a great opportunity for anybody contemplat-
ing a few marriages at some future time. Three of the rings
went for eighty dollars, one bringing thirty and the other two
going for twenty-five apiece. Those twenty-five dollar jobs
would have been handy for a marrying man like Tommy Man-
ville, and the thirty-dollar circlet would have done for something a little more lasting; but the diamond-encrusted band for
which a gentleman bidder paid fifteen hundred and twenty-
five dollars was never intended for a leisurely trip to Reno.
That ring was surely made to have and to hold. One wonders
if it did, or possibly still does. One of the rings, we are told,
went to a certain Mrs. I. D. who had been married for twenty-
six years to a sculptor, who, she explained had been too busy to

buy her a wedding ring. She bid in one herself for thirty dollars.

Among other surplus articles sold that day was Hedy's over-sized bed, described by the auctioneer as a "conversation piece." With some amusement and a few raised eyebrows it went to a forty-year-old aircraft supply dealer for two hundred and fifty dollars. This gorgeous piece of bedroom furniture with a diamond-set headboard and a rose velvet spread was bought allegedly for a three-and-a-half-year-old child because she was thought by her parents to resemble Hedy. A Steinway grand piano went to a song writer for twenty-four hundred dollars after he had entertained the thousand assembled visitors with several of Hedy's favorite selections.

Beds of screen personalities often bring out entertaining persiflage when put up for sale at auction. Such an event occurred at the sale of a bed belonging to Barbara Stanwyck which a Beverly Hills decorator finally won with a bid of three hundred and sixty dollars. When the buyer stepped up to pay the bill the cashier gave him a sly wink. "For that money," he said, "you ought to get the lady, too."

"I'm not buying it for myself," the purchaser snapped, "and my client wants it not on account of glamour, but because of its good design."

The cashier shook his head skeptically. "Never knew any-one to have good designs on a bed," he muttered as he rang up the check.

During the auctioning of the personal effects of John Barry-more, a large pink girdle was bought by a paunchy businessman who announced to the audience that he was buying it "just as a memento," which brought down the house.

At a Hollywood auction in 1952 a "regie" book—the manu-script used in preparing a production for shooting, and con-taining the notes and comments of the director—came up for sale at the Goldenberg Auction Galleries. The director in this case happened to be the famous Max Reinhardt, perhaps the most prominent theatrical figure of all Europe. Naturally the greats of Hollywood were there in force and academic circles from all over the state were well represented. Both UCLA and SC were out to get the notes if possible, but they decided not to cut each other's throat and patched up a truce by the terms of which SC was to handle the bidding. To be doubly sure SC decided to send in a professional to do the bidding and hired Jake Zeitlin, a rare book dealer, to attend the auction and "pick up the material."

But it was not quite so easy as all that, for Zeitlin ran into determined competition from none other than Marilyn Monroe. There were plenty of other bidders but they did not last long when they learned the identity of their competitors, and quickly dropped out and left Zeitlin and the actress to fight it out between them. As Zeitlin explained it afterward, Marilyn came up with the best figure and walked off with the prize for a bid of $1,335.

Greatly annoyed when it was hinted that she had made the purchase as a publicity stunt, she declared emphatically that publicity had not received any consideration whatever in the transaction, and explained that she was well aware of the value of the work sheets to students of the drama and was concerned about obtaining all 178 of them because she had been informed that otherwise they would have been sold singly and the set broken up and scattered. She further explained that she had been told that several colleges including Harvard were interested in acquiring them, and after looking over the field she had decided to present the work sheets to "that school."

More than 5,000 antiques had been auctioned off at the Old World Galleries of Henry D. Meyer on North Vine Street in Hollywood, a favorite hangout of Motion Picture people during their leisure hours, when after twenty-eight years of auctioneering Henry felt his voice failing and decided to retire. According to the old vendue-master, the most important articles he had sold under the hammer in all those years were, first, a bed in which Napoleon had slept; and second, the old-fashioned tub in which Merle Oberon had bathed while playing a part in the film version of *Wuthering Heights*.

It is not unusual to have a crowd running into the thousands when the furnishings of some prominent film star come up for auction and often as many as 10,000 will visit the preview, which usually lasts for two or three days. This is especially true of the auction sale of furs which have been worn in some of the big successful million-dollar productions. Although these garments are specially designed for the particular picture in which they are used, they belong not to the studio but to a firm of furriers whose sole business is the making and renting of furs to the various studios. For garments which may be worth as much as ten or twenty thousand dollars can be used for a single picture, after which they must be entirely re-designed.

The furs may be reassembled and made over into a different style any number of times until the furs begin to show wear, but no fur garment as such can go before the camera more than once. The artists themselves do no worrying about the furs, for the studios have to pay the rentals for the fur garments which are originally designed, collected, and made for a particular artist in a particular part of a particular play. So striking are some of these garments that if used in a second production, even by a different studio and against a totally different background, they would be instantly recognized by the audience, and there would be a significant nodding of heads and whispering behind hands that the company must be in trouble or it wouldn't be using secondhand costumes; and the star must be slipping or she would never stand for such an indignity.

These auctions of the film furs may take place in either California or New York, though the furriers prefer New York because they get better prices there. Curiously enough, the buyers at the fur auctions either in California or New York, though intensely critical of some of the things they see on the screen, are inordinately proud to be seen wearing furs that have graced some of the world's most gorgeous and enchanting women, and they are not at all backward about boasting of the fact that the coats or capes or stoles or whatever have been before the camera and were bought at a great reduction—this in spite of the fact that the principal charm of mink, broadtail, silver fox or chinchilla is that it is notable for its costliness.

Another thing that impressionable people are inclined to brag about is any souvenir that has belonged to a Hollywood star, a cigarette holder, a key chain, a vanity case, any little personal trinket. These things are eagerly contested for at auctions, and are as often as not fraudulent.

Perhaps the most spectacular auction of the personal effects of a screen personality was that of a young Italian boy whose original ambition was to become a gardener. His name was Rudolph Alfonzo Raffaele Piere Filebert Gugliemi di Valitina d'Antonguolla known as Rudolph Valentino. However, Rudolph was not present at his own auction, for he had previously departed this life at the New York Polyclinic Hospital with only two white-capped nurses at his bedside while thousands of weeping women jammed the streets outside and defied a cordon of police to open a passage to traffic.

Resting in a plain wicker basket which might have carried soiled laundry, though covered with a cloth of gold, his body was removed from the back door of the hospital and taken to a funeral home a few blocks away. Here some thirty thousand frantic females along with a few disgruntled males congregated despite the efforts of the police to drive them away; and when an attempt was made to allow a public view of the body lying in state, rioters burst in the doors breaking a cathedral glass window and battled to reach the body which was resting on a catafalque in the Gold Room. Scores of the rioters and numerous policemen were taken to the hospital seriously injured, and at the height of the turmoil the screams and moans of the rioters could be heard blocks away.

When finally the parlors were cleared and placed under an army of police, a detachment of ten Fascisti all dressed in black appeared with telegraphic orders from Mussolini to act as a guard of honor through the night. In spite of the effrontery, they were admitted and took over the sentry duty until morning. Lines were established and further disorder prevented for the time being.

With all this publicity to work with Valentino's manager skilfully arranged a funeral cortege with top Hollywood mourners when the body was removed for shipment to California. When workmen went to clean up the broken glass from the cathedral window not so much as a shard could be found, even the tiniest fragment having been carried off by souvenir hunters. The draped funeral car passed slowly across the country as if it carried the remains of a deceased president; but the railroad authorities at Chicago wisely avoided any danger of emotional excesses by switching it around the city although crowds of distraught females waited at the station all day weeping silently or sighing.

Up to this time Valentino's ex-wives had been very much in evidence, bringing gifts and flowers and granting interviews which were punctuated with occasional pompous telegrams from relatives now on their way from Europe, for they were already quarreling over his estate, not knowing that he had died deeply in debt. However, so cleverly had Valentino's manager handled his publicity that a prompt reissue of the most important of the Valentino films was to put his estate hundreds of thousands of dollars to the good and give the family something really worth fighting for.

Hollywood met the funeral train as it would have met that of any other important film personality. There was no such general tear-letting as there had been in New York or Chicago. The film folk went to the funeral as they would have attended an opening. They went largely to see what was going on and who was there; and there may have been some of the sense of duty which usually drags people to funerals. Hollywood may be sentimental, but it is also hard-boiled, and such tears as were shed came largely from impressionable females who knew Valentino only as a picture they had seen on the screen.

Among incidental happenings of the obsequies one woman committed suicide for love of the beautiful young man, and another attempted suicide unsuccessfully but received equal publicity, lacking only the obituary notices. Probate matters, of course, had to wait the arrival of relatives who had started posthaste for Hollywood upon learning of Valentino's death.

When eventually the relatives arrived, great crowds thronged into the Hall of Arts for the opening of the series of auctions for the disposition of Valentino's personal effects; but it was an audience of sightseers and sensation hunters. Indeed, during the opening sessions they showed so little interest in bidding that the auctioneers were loath to offer any but the most inconsequential items for sale, or if they did try to dispose of anything of worth they would place the initial bid so high as to discourage those who might have been inclined to make a reasonable offer and thus start normal bidding.

However, when the public began to read in the papers that theaters all over the country and even in England were contesting fiercely for the rights to show the reisssued films of the deceased actor, the returns from which were destined to run into the millions, the bidding at the Valentino auctions went soaring upward. The noted gold and cashmere shawl seen at the funeral brought $2,925, and Valentino's Italian piano, though somewhat battered, was quickly bid up to $2,100. Bebe Daniels, after a spirited contest with an antique dealer, paid $1,000 for a collection of antique firearms.

One of the keenest contests during the auctions arose over the famous Valentino power cruiser which had long been furnishing romantic gossip all up and down the neighboring coastline from Half Moon Bay to Coronado, which finally went up as high as $2,100. The totals of the sale were not given to the public, but they must have been eminently satisfactory to the family. Indeed, the only item which might have been regarded as a bargain was a large portrait of the actor which had cost him many weary hours of sitting and $6,000 in money. This went for only $400.

Nor was it, as had been predicted, bid in by Pola Negri who was rumored to be engaged to Rudolph before he met his untimely death. Quite the contrary, for while his estate was in process of settlement she filed a bill for $15,000 and interest on a note for money she had loaned him for the purpose of building a house.

CHAPTER FOURTEEN

"FINDS"

MANY PEOPLE GO TO AUCTIONS LOOKING FOR BARGAINS. PERHAPS most people do. And a few go because they are in need of a particular article and don't want to spend the money for a new one. Then of course there are those who go entirely for the entertainment, and I know one young couple who go looking for "finds."

They have in their lovely old colonial home up in the Shepaug neighborhood of New England everything they could possibly need in the way of antique furnishings, and not a stick or splinter of it was handed down to them. They collected it all; and in the process they developed a serious case of collectivitis. They simply couldn't stay away from a good auction even if they knew in advance there was nothing there of the slightest interest to them in the way of merchandise. They used to say they went to watch the people, for auctions do bring out all sorts and conditions of men, to say nothing of the women and children who can't help heeding the call when the voice of the auctioneer is heard in the land.

In the city the women are likely to go smartly dressed, but in the country they go to an auction looking as if they had dressed for a fire. I once saw a rather pretty young woman sitting calmly in the midst of an auction wrapped in a crazy quilt, and when I chanced to observe a naked kneecap I suspected that the quilt was all. That was wishful thinking for it turned out that the lady was wearing shorts. My friends from Shepaug were always well dressed at an auction, for which they excused themselves on the ground that they might want to buy something expensive and they wanted to look as if their credit rating was good. They became familiar with all sorts of auction oddities. They knew a slub at sight, and could tell a rollipoke without even feeling it; but one day when they were attending a sale in a small country town Cindy, the wife, gently touched the elbow of Bill, the husband, and called his attention to a curious-looking object lying on the auctioneer's table.

Bill squinted at the thing, for he hated to admit that there was anything likely to be seen at an auction that he could not identify, but he finally shook his head and intimated that he didn't know. At just that moment a sudden downpour of rain came swishing in at the windows and most of those who were not leaping up to get away from the spray or struggling to close the windows were rushing outside to close the windows of their cars or put up the tops, and almost instantly the auction was a scene of the utmost confusion.

It so happened, however, that Bill and Cindy had already closed the windows of their car fearing that it might rain, and since they were sitting nowhere near the windows there was no danger of their getting wet. Bill who made a practice of being calm in emergencies, moved quietly over to the auctioneer's table and examined the strange object which had aroused their curiosity.

He found it to be a thin piece of wood about the size and shape of a palmleaf fan only much more substantially made. It had obviously been sawed out of a single board, and Bill's first impression was that it would have made a good ping-pong paddle for an unskilled player. Bill had never seen anything like it before. The face of it which was ten or twelve inches across was covered with printing in Old American letters. About the first thing he deciphered was the Lord's Prayer. Then he noticed the days of the week, the names of the months, the four seasons, and the letters of the alphabet with the vowels indicated by being colored in red. He did not have time to examine further and returned to his seat more puzzled than when he had left it. They had intended to go as soon as the rain stopped, but now they decided to stay long enough to see what happened to the strange object.

They had not long to wait, for it was the first thing the auctioneer took in his hand when he returned to the rostrum. He held it up and waved it aloft as he asked. "What am I offered for this thing?"

He didn't even know what it was. People laughed and the auctioneer, who was a bit of a smarty, turned to the owner who had found it among some rubbish in his attic. "Will you be kind enough to tell me what this thing is?" he asked.

The owner smiled. "I have been told that it was made for a child's primer," he said. "In the olden days before the printing press it was called a *hornbook*."

"A hornbook, eh?" said the auctioneer. "All right, what am I offered for this hornbook?"

Somebody started it at a dollar, and at the pressure on his arm from Cindy, Bill raised the bid to two dollars. There was no great enthusiasm, and after a few small bids they had it. On the way home they kept talking about it, not realizing how valuable it was, but tickled with themselves for finding a relic so unusual. It was not until they had looked it up in the encyclopedia that they began to appreciate that they had made a real find—that is, if it was genuine.

The hornbooks described by the authorities were made the same way except that the lettering was done on paper or parchment which was pasted on the wood and protected by a covering of horn scraped so thin as to be transparent. "But," adds the encyclopedist, "there are few existing specimens known." *Bri-*

tannica goes on to say that the hornbook was usually strung by the handle and hung at the child's girdle, and also that it often contained a large cross and was called "Christ-cross-row" and latterly "criss-cross-row."

When the young find-hunters took it to an antiquarian for appraisal he said it was undoubtedly genuine, but he refused to put a price on it, saying that it was priceless and had no place in a private collection, but should rightfully be in a museum where it could be seen, studied, and enjoyed by generations to come. So they presented it to one of the great museums where it has since been on exhibition; and they will tell you that they sleep better at night for not having the responsibility for keeping it in their own home.

Their second find came to them by proxy. They were having some carpentry done on their house, and since the nearest and best workman lived some distance away, they followed the local custom of having him "live in" while working for them, and he was a guest they thoroughly enjoyed. He was a folksy fellow and if you went anywhere near him while he was at work he would lay down his tools and settle down for a half hour's chat. The only way Bill could get away was to start a good long sentence and then keep walking until he was out of hearing distance.

The carpenter simply could not understand why Bill and Cindy would go to auctions and pay more for old things than new ones would cost; and like a real Yankee, he did not hesitate to say so. He would pick up a piece of Ironstone china and look at it shaking his head. They used it for kitchen china at his house and not on their dining-room table. And that old mirror in the bathroom with the glass so crooked you couldn't tell whether you were looking at yourself or somebody else, and paying forty dollars for it when you could get one in New Milford for two fifty that would make your reflection look like a photograph.

There was nothing mean or disagreeable about it; he was just puzzled and he knew them well enough to do a little joshing. But Bill and Cindy insisted that he was one of the most delightful guests they had ever entertained. It was several weeks after he had finished the job and left that he came rattling into the yard one day in his old panel truck, and without shutting off the engine hurried up to Bill who was working over one of the flowerbeds, and held out a substantial-sized manilla envelope.

"Got a C.O.D. present for you," he said with a grin. "It'll cost you ten cents—just what it cost me. Got it over to Sweedler's auction. Mine was the only bid, because nobody wants an old atlas—not as old as this—nobody but you. Got a dime on you?"

Bill gave him a dime. "I'll take it from you sight unseen," he said. "With anybody else I'd have to see it before parting with any money."

"You mean it might not be old enough?" the carpenter shouted back over his shoulder as he hurried to his truck. "Say hello to the Missus for me!" And he went rattling off.

The present turned out to be a *Carey's American Atlas* published in 1795 and still in perfect condition. It had some beautiful maps of early New England and a map of the United States with one of the states missing. But since the gift was bought at an auction, Bill and Cindy have scored it as a find and several of the maps are now framed and hanging on their walls.

Their next find was a chest which they bid in for thirty-five dollars. It was not in good repair, but there was a nobility about the primitive carving on it that made them believe in its quality. They took some tracings of the carving and some small pieces of wood that had come loose and submitted them to the curator of the American Wing of the Metropolitan Museum of Art. He was much impressed with the exhibits and sent them to an expert antiquarian located nearby who pronounced the chest the product of some Frisian craftsmen who had settled in America soon after the landing of the Pilgrims, and placed the date of the chest at about 1638. When they asked him the probable value he said that in better condition it would be worth considerably more, but even in its present state he considered it to be worth at least $1,400.

These things are happening frequently wherever auctions are being held, which is practically everywhere. The auctioneers don't always know about them. Of course they knew about the one where at the end of the auction they sold the kitchen table the cashier had been using for a desk. It went for only a dollar or two, but some time after it had been taken away the cashier remembered that all the day's receipts were in the table drawer. And the law is that, unless expressly reserved, the contents go to the buyer with the container. That same law applied in Philadelphia where a man bid in a filing cabinet for only a dollar or two and on reaching home discovered that one of the drawers was full of old papers among which he found the original documents for the incorporation of the city of Philadelphia, to recover which the city had to pay $550.

Some auctioneers go in for "Klondikes" large or small just to get an auction started and let people try out their voices. Sometimes these are arranged ahead of time by filling baskets, boxes, and buckets. And again the auction starts with the empty receptacle into which the auctioneer puts one object after another, as a means of getting acquainted with his audience. "Ladies and gentlemen, let's start off today with something useful—this splendid split-hickory basket, sound in every strand," he taps it with the handle of his hammer. "Just the thing to carry home the garden tools you'll be buying today, for with this fine spring weather we'll all be wanting to make our gardens. Here's a trowel to soften up the soil," he drops it in. "And a dibble to help you plant your seeds," he drops that in. "And a spud to dig out the stubborn weeds left over from last season," he also drops that in. "And here you are all ready to start your garden—what am I offered?" He swings the basket back and forth for all to see. "All you need is the seeds and you're ready to go. Do I hear a dollar—? Do I hear fifty cents just to start the ball rolling—?"

One day in Westport I saw a woman buy a basket because she wanted a basket, and she was somewhat annoyed when the helper handed it to her to discover that it had some old newspapers in the bottom, and not too clean at that; but when she went to throw the newspapers away she found underneath two lacy-glass Sandwich cup plates worth fifteen dollars apiece.

But it is among the old books, and especially among the old paintings that some of the greatest finds are discovered. The country auctioneer ordinarily knows nothing about either and golden opportunities are likely to slip through his fingers every time he sells a stack of old books or struggles to get five dollars for a grimy old painting with half the gilt knocked off the frame. Furniture and household effects he understands perfectly; farm animals and implements he knows at a glance, but the touch of an artist's brush or the smell of printer's ink is a complete blank to him, and if they come into his shop unknown they pass out the same way and he doesn't even know they have been there. Imagine finding at a country auction in Maine a copy of the rare first edition of Hawthorne's *Fanshawe*, a volume worth considerably over a thousand dollars, which was found in the bottom of a bean pot sold to a housewife who bid it in for fifty cents with the intention of cooking beans in it?

It was also up in Maine—or down Maine if you prefer—that a copy of *Tamerlane and Other Poems*, Poe's first book, sold at auction for a dollar. Of course Poe's name was not on it. The timorous youth of eighteen would not hear of such a thing. The book—or rather the paper-cover pamphlet—was published in 1827 under the *nom de plume* of "A. Bostonian." The public was not aware of the value of the book at the time, nor did it become aware until Vincent Starrett wrote for the *Saturday Evening Post* in 1925 an article on old and rare books called

"Have You a Tamerlane in Your Attic?" intimating that if you had you could sell it for at least $10,000. Whereupon an elderly lady living in an attic in Worcester produced a copy which was bid in by Owen D. Young for $17,500 and is now owned by the New York Public Library. Another copy of *Tamerlane* was sold for $31,000. And if you are not too busy at the moment you might take a look in your own attic.

It is the same with paintings by almost any of the Old Masters. Only months ago a story appeared in *The New York Times* with a dateline of Madrid, Spain, about a Spaniard who bought for $38.40 an old picture he had been seeing for years in the dusty window of a decrepit antique shop. He had once priced it, but the dealer wanted 10,000 pesetas which the would-be customer thought far too high (in our money $256). Chancing to see it at auction four years later he was able to buy it for $38.46. But by this time it had become so filthy that he sent it to be cleaned.

He did not recognize it when it returned from the cleaners, and felt sure that another picture had been substituted. However, he changed his tune when experts were called in and pronounced it an unknown work by Murillo, the noted Spanish painter who died in 1682—and valued at many thousands of dollars. Its genuineness was easily established.

But it is not necessary to go so far afield for the "find" of a valuable painting, several of them, in fact, for they exist here in our own country. In the spring of 1956 a story broke in the New York papers with a headline:

$150,000 PAINTINGS
SOLD AS BARGAINS
Two in Set of Four
Brought Only $40 Two
Years Ago at Conn-
ecticut Sale

The story goes on to tell how two decorative panels which had been picked up at a New England auction two years before were to be united with a pair from which they had been separated for a quarter of a century. The four, it was asserted by New York art authorities, if put on the market now would bring upwards of $150,000. And despite the fact that the two pairs were in the hands of different dealers, it was stated on reliable authority that a joint exhibition and auction sale was being arranged for the early future.

These strikingly brilliant panels were commissioned in 1914 by Edwin R. Campbell, one of the founders of the Chevrolet Company, for the foyer of his apartment at 635 Park Avenue, New York. Wassily Kandinsky, the Russian artist employed, was little known in this country at the time, though he was a gifted painter. The specifications for the panels called for a height of sixty-four inches and varying widths from thirty-one to forty-eight inches to fit the space. All four were signed with the initial "K" and dated 1916. The initial cost of the four panels was $469.20.

When finished the panels hung in the Park Avenue apartment until 1921 when Mr. Campbell moved with his family to his Palm Beach home in Florida where he died in 1929.

Subsequently when the Florida house was sold the two large panels were bought by an artist named Murray Hoffman. But unfortunately Hoffman's wife had taken a strong dislike to the abstract tendency and stubbornly refused to allow the panels to be hung in their home, so again the paintings went into the attic—and Hoffman had the white elephant on his hands. However, while on a visit to New York he saw some of the later work of Kandinsky who had by this time thrown himself vigorously into the modern abstract expressionist movement and Hoffman, seeing an opportunity to unload his white elephant, placed the two panels with an auction gallery in New York where they brought $400. This was only a little find. It is the buyer who will make the big one, for the panels, now valued up in the thousands, are increasing in value every day.

And in the meantime the smaller panels after a lengthy storage in the Florida house found their way back North and eventually turned up at an auction in New England where one was sold for $25 and the other for only $15. As the auctioneer tells the story, the woman who had bought the cheaper panel probably doubled her money when she sold it to a New York dealer, for she hurried back to New England and bought the $25 panel from the other bidder, probably paying $50 or less, and promptly sold it to the same dealer for $100.

It was the chagrined auctioneer who had sold the panels for a song who gave me the figures. "I don't know whether the present owner knows what a find he's got," he said regretfully. "He prob'ly does if he reads the papers, for those panels have had a lot of publicity. Take it from me, the Kandinsky market is on the way up, and if he'll just sit tight and hold fast he'll make himself a handsome profit—that could just as well have been mine if I'd only had more brains and a little mite of good luck."

Bidders aren't the only ones who make finds, for occasionally the auctioneer himself uncovers a pleasant surprise. Some years ago O. Rundle Gilbert, a famous auctioneer who lives in the Hudson Valley, received a telephone call from a New York trust company with whom he frequently works, asking him to dispose of a small house and contents in Garrison, New York, for the purpose of settling an estate, the kind of task which often comes to an auctioneer. The rub was that it wasn't much of a job since the entire property had been appraised by the family at only $600. Hardly worth bothering with, they said, but it was holding back the settlement of the estate, and it would be a great favor to the company and the family as well if he would take care of the matter. Just get rid of it, they said, and don't spend too much money doing it.

It turned out to be an old house which had been used as a

studio by a well-known portrait painter named Robert W. Weir, former art instructor at West Point, while engaged in painting some historical pictures for the rotunda of the Capitol in Washington, the most famous of which is "The Embarkation of the Pilgrims," a picture well known to every visitor to the Capitol, which was in all probability painted in this little six-hundred-dollar house. The only furniture in the place, the auctioneer was told, was some old junk pieces picked up in the neighborhood by the artist for use as settings in his historical pictures.

With this idea in his mind Mr. Gilbert turned the key in the lock and forced open the door creaking on its rusty hinges. The first thing he saw inside the house was a three-tier game table which in spite of its coat of dust he instantly recognized as a valuable antique. His next find was a Chippendale drop-leaf table and a number of Chippendale dining chairs. Nearby was a Martha Washington chair, still sound though in need of refinishing, and there were other things.

At first he was puzzled at the presence of these obviously valuable pieces in the rickety little old house, until it came to him that when the artist had picked them up in the neighborhood for a virtual song they were not yet antiques, for nobody was collecting antiques back in the 1840's when the paintings were being done. At that time they were such discarded pieces as were probably to be found in every attic in the neighborhood.

Properly displayed at a well-advertised auction the so-called "junk furniture" brought over $18,000.

In 1918 with the world depressed and war-weary after four years of conflict and desolation a small painting 29 by 26 inches in size was sold in London for twenty-eight guineas, then worth about eighty dollars. It was called "An Allegory of Prudence" and was quite obviously an old-timer. It was believed by some people to be a Titian, possibly done in his later years when his eyes were dim and his hands shaky for he lived to the ripe old age of ninety-nine years, and continued painting up to the last.

The upper part of the design shows the heads of an old man, a middle-aged man in the prime of life, and a youth; in the lower part are a wolf, a lion, and a dog. Nobody fully understood quite what it meant, but it had a curious appeal, and since the price was low it was bought by somebody willing to take a gamble.

Just where it had been during the forty intervening years the brief newspaper report does not say. But somehow it had found its way into the private collection of the late Francis Howard, and when it recently came on the market at Christie's it was immediately recognized as a long-lost Titian and went on the auction block as a genuine find where it was sold under the hammer for 11,000 guineas ($32,340) and is just starting its career as a find some 340 and possibly 400 years after it was painted.

Another notable find has recently been made in England, a resounding discovery of an estimated value of $560,000, in an old family collection, an experience that comes to few collectors among their own pictures, especially when the picture was originally bought for a mere token value of 100 pounds as late as 1845, having at that time been falsely credited to the Italian painter, Giovanni Francesco Caroto, instead of Albrecht Dürer, the famous German artist.

It could easily have been overlooked for it is a tiny picture only 8½ by 6¼ inches and is painted on a panel of pearwood depicting St. Jerome in a brilliant blue robe kneeling before a crucifix in the wilderness. This discovery is regarded as one of the most important art finds made in Britain in many years.

The painting which had been lying unrecognized all these years in the splendid collection of Sir Edmund Bacon, Premier Baronet of England, having been purchased by one of his ancestors, was only recently recognized from a chance photograph which happened to fall into the hands of an expert who immediately identified the Dürer technique.

Sir Edward, who is a director of Lloyd's Bank, has announced that he has no intention of selling his newly-discovered find, remarking that too many beautiful things had already left England.

CHAPTER FIFTEEN

SOTHEBY'S

Auction sales of art and literature came to England from the Dutch, being known in Leyden and Amsterdam as early as 1604, and were common occurrences there during the period while the Pilgrims were self-exiled in Holland. However, it was not until 1676 that one William Cooper, a venturesome London bookseller living at the sign of the Pelican, had the first auction sale of books ever held in England.

It was not a howling success, but it was a beginning. The idea spread slowly, and having established the fact that books could be successfully sold under the hammer, paintings, prints, porcelains, jewels, and other objects of art timorously followed, and in course of time outsold the books and eventually came to dominate the great auction houses.

All this was a gradual development and almost a century and a half had passed since the initial auction by Cooper before Samuel Baker of Russell Street, Covent Garden, opened an auction gallery for the sale of all the objects of art contrived by man, thereby establishing his firm, currently known as Sotheby's, as the first in England to engage in that occupation.

It goes without saying that the business was not a runaway

success. It prospered so slowly that twenty-three years had passed before it was enough of a success to take in as a partner a certain George Leigh. The partnership, however, was not of long duration, for Baker soon retired from the business and went to live in a villa at Chigwell in Essex. A picture painted by Grigner at this time shows Baker to have been a sedate but determined-looking old gentleman in a white bob-wig and a plum-colored coat. His auctioneer's gavel has recently been retired after nearly two centuries of service to the status of exhibit.

It was not until the year of Baker's death that his nephew, John Sotheby, joined the firm with Leigh bringing the name of Sotheby into the partnership and changing the firm name to Baker, Leigh & Sotheby. In 1861 the last of the Sothebys died and John Wilkenson, who had previously come into the partnership, was soon joined by Edward Grose Hodge and from 1861 to 1924 the firm went under the name and style of Sotheby, Wilkinson & Hodge. From time to time other distinguished partners came and tarried and passed on, but in 1924 the firm name of Sotheby & Company was adopted and has remained the same to the present time.

The business of the book and art auctioneer is one which sounds wonderful until you try it, says one of the Sotheby executives, who further adds that the long career of Sotheby's is strewn with the wrecks of once successful competitors. Evans, who sold the famous Roxburghe library, and Robbins, whose catalogue of the contents of Strawberry Hill reached the "all-time peak of magniloquent irrelevance," are but two who failed to make the grade. Of those founded in the eighteenth century only Sotheby's, the earliest, and Christie's, dating from 1763, along with the auction rooms established in 1776 at 38 King Street, Covent Garden, by Samuel Paterson, have survived with one or two others into the present century.

At the turn of the century Sotheby's, which had been largely concentrating on books, was riding the crest of the wave and handling a large porportion of the great book collections coming into the market, such as the libraries of Talleyrand, of Napoleon I, of Jerome Bonaparte, and the collection of the King of Holland, consigned by his nephew who became Napoleon III. These were quickly followed by three other great collections which brought a total of more than a million pounds, being the Britwell Library, the Huth collection, and the Phillipps library —the latter famous for having been in course of disposal for sixty-seven years.

It was at this time that Sotheby's, which had long been located on Wellington Street, Strand, where the firm had moved in 1818, concluded that the area was no longer suitable for their growing business and made a daring decision to move to the West End into much larger quarters and put greater emphasis on works of art in the widest possible field. They were by no means strangers in the field of fine arts, and had in the heydey of "Academy" art sold a fair proportion of the contemporary output. But for the handling of the great art sales of Old Masters and the like they had never previously been properly housed and equipped.

At the new location, however, they naturally expected a fair increase in business, but they were hardly prepared for the tenfold enlargement in business which occurred in the succeeding years; nor did they anticipate that book sales would decrease to no more than 10 per cent of the total business.

One of the first great art sales in the new location consisted of a collection of the paintings, engravings, and armor of Lord Pembroke, which aggregated about one hundred thousand pounds and included the famous jacob suit of Henry Herbert, Earl of Pembroke. This was bid in for an American client, Mr. Clarence Mackay, for twenty-five thousand pounds and is now standing in the Metropolitan Museum in New York City where it is much admired by gangsters and thugs as well as the makers of bulletproof vests and armored trucks.

The opulent period of the late 1920's during which many of the Sotheby's house records were broken, saw a notable revival in the sale of books, which had for some time been in the doldrums. The year 1927 completed the long-drawn-out disposal of the Phillipps library with a return of nearly six hundred and fifty thousand pounds, including a single session of one hundred and ten thousand pounds, a world's record long unbroken.

Then came the Halford sale which brought ninety-five thousand pounds, followed by the selling of the Lutrell Psalter and Bedford Hours at more than sixty-four thousand pounds, and the collection of Americana gathered by Henry Percy, Ninth Earl of Northumberland, who from a prison cell backed some of the earliest ventures in American colonization.

Another important and somewhat unusual occurrence was the sale of the contents of the Lord Rothschild house in Piccadilly for a total of one hundred and twenty-five thousand pounds before a large crowd which watched with amusement the keen rivalry between the Dutch and the French collectors who nearly came to blows over their bidding, both being as noted as the Scots for their canny deals.

On Hitler's rise to power some of the large collectors in France, fearing the worst, began to seek cover by unloading some of their choicest objects of art at the London sales. Adrien Fauchier, a wealthy Paris banker, placed with Sotheby's a collection of ninety-nine small paintings which brought some eighty thousand pounds; and the Compte de Greffulhe sent over some beautiful odds and ends which went for sixty-two thousand pounds. Even the non-Aryan collectors in Germany managed to slip through the Nazi curtain—at a terrific cost in

bribery no doubt—such of their art treasures as were incon-
spicuous enough to have a chance of getting through.

In 1938 after a long-continued exodus of great collections
and after numerous examples of old and rare books had crossed
to America for sale, the tide turned momentarily when the
splendid library of the late Mortimer Schiff came to Sotheby's
for sale and was hailed by the London press as the first of the
great American collections to cross the ocean from west to
east in many years. It was hoped that this was the beginning
of a trend. But as it failed to meet with any notable success,
bringing only fifty thousand pounds—and as it was followed
almost immediately by the second World War, any possibility
of a trend died a-borning.

Though the coming of the war did not, as in 1914, close the
doors of the auction galleries, it did reduce their transactions to
an inconsiderable minimum, for a large proportion of the art
treasures were removed from the galleries to places of safety
from the fiendish bombing of the Nazis from the sky and even
from continental bomb sites which hurled their robot missiles
across the Channel.

In the spring of 1940, however, there was held at Sotheby's
a sale of the residue of the great Eumorfopolus collection of
Chinese art, which proved to be a godsend to French collectors,
whose buying orders in early June were among the last commercial messages sent over the cross-channel cables before the
hobnailed boots of the German invaders were heard tramping
the pavements of undefended Paris.

France was liberated in the summer of 1944, but Germany
held out stubbornly in the homeland until the spring of 1945;
and it was not until the A-bomb fell on Hiroshima the following summer that it was all over but the shouting. Down came
the shutters, and up went the shades, and once more the world
could draw a normal breath. Out came the art treasures from

the mines, caves, vaults, and other holes in the ground where they had been hidden, and once more they were on display in the museums, galleries, and auction houses.

The art market after the late war was as active as in 1918-1920, though limited largely to British home collections. London sales of European collections which at Sotheby's alone had been worked up to half a million pounds during prewar years, had practically ceased to exist, even after peace was restored. This was because of the wartime exchange control and the unrealistic import and export regulations. Sotheby's, which had more or less specialized in this foreign trade, was under extreme pressure until a specially licensed sale from Florence brought in some ninety-one thousand pounds; and the sale of the Dyson Perrim's books added another hundred and forty-eight thousand, including twenty-two thousand paid for one of the two volumes of a Gutenberg Bible.

There was little general prosperity in the big auction galleries, however, until December of 1954 when the government lifted the currency regulations and allowed imported works of art and antiques to be paid for in the currency of the nation from which they were received instead of requiring all such payments to be made in pounds. This opened the head gates. Foreign dealers came flocking in and soon the boom was on.

For many years the English had been worrying over the one-way traffic in objects of art from Britain to America, and the depletion of the art collections in the great country houses of the British Isles. There had been oratory in Parliament about it, but until the currency regulations little was done to put a stop to it except the appointment of a reviewing committee set up in 1952, which was empowered to stop the export of any work of art by reimbursing a foreign buyer with the amount of his purchase and adding the work of art in question to one of Britain's nationally owned collections.

Had this arrangement been strictly adhered to it might soon have put an end to the remunerative art business of the auction houses of Britain; but the government has always been tight-fisted about its purchases for the national galleries, and in addition there have been recent indications that the drift of art treasures from Britain to America is not so much of a one-way stream as had been supposed, for the great Weinberg sale recently held at Sotheby's has, to quote the *Illustrated London News*, "strikingly confirmed London's place as a leading centre of the world's art market."

The London *Times* refers to the Weinberg auction as "the most outstanding sale of paintings in recent years" and hails it as a "firm indication that London has fully regained its position as an art dealing centre."

Incidentally, Herr Weinberg was a Dutch banker from Amsterdam who had settled in Scarsdale, New York, and had spent much of his lifetime making a collection of nineteenth-century and modern paintings and bronzes, having a special affinity for Impressionist and Postimpressionist pieces. Just how his collection happened to be placed on sale in London rather than in New York or Philadelphia has not been divulged; but starting with a single Corot he amassed what is said to have been one of the most notable collections of modern art ever assembled. And this it was which went under the hammer at the auction rooms of Sotheby & Company at 34 New Bond Street on July 10, 1957, at "eleven o'clock precisely."

Coming so soon after the great excitement in Paris over the Biddle sale of Gauguin's "Still Life with Apples" for nearly three hundred thousand dollars,* the Weinberg sale aroused an intense interest in London and everywhere else in the world where the meaning of the word "art" is understood. Everybody was talking about it and nobody who could possibly get there

---

* June 14th, 1957, reported in Chapter 20.

failed to show up. Even the Queen, who is not ordinarily known as a patron of the arts, added greatly to the public interest by making an evening visit to Sotheby's with the Duke of Edinburgh and Princess Margaret a day or two before the sale, thus showing what a tizzy dear old London was in over the skyrocketing prices of art that could hardly be given away a generation ago.

It is safe to say that there were some hastily-eaten luncheons that July day in London with the opening of the sale scheduled at "eleven o'clock precisely." And at that, Mollie Panter-Downs, reporting for the *New Yorker*, puts the opening at two minutes *after* eleven precisely when Mr. Peter Wilson ascended the rostrum and asked for an opening bid of one hundred pounds for three small bronze figures by Daumier.

He received it and more after it, but it was like the warm-up pitches at a ball game—it didn't mean very much to the breathless crowds who were jammed into the various rooms of the galleries where a large proportion of those who succeeded in getting inside the doors were receiving their thrills over the closed circuit television for which a screen had been set up in each of the crowded rooms of the establishment.

But these outriders were far from being mere television viewers. All the rooms were equipped for making bids which were instantly relayed to the rostrum by an assistant auctioneer with an open circuit telephone; and numerous sales were made to bidders who were not even in the same room with the pictures they were buying—at the price of an oil man's ransom.

The first of the paintings to go into the big money was a Cézanne—a portrait of the artist's wife—which brought fourteen thousand pounds and will return to America since it was purchased for an American client. Next to go skyward was one of Mr. Weinberg's Corots, and after that there were two pictures by Degas followed by a Fantin-Latours floral piece.

Next came a Gauguin of two naked urchins which went for seventeen thousand pounds.

There was a flurry of excitement when the porters held up Renoir's "Jeune Femme au Corsage Rouge" turning it this way and that for all to see—just as the handlers at a prize fight hold up a huge numeral so patrons may be sure of the round coming up. It's an old English custom and must traditionally be done before placing the canvas on the easel. As in real life the photographers pressed forward to get a shot of the fascinating young girl—whose portrait fetched twenty-two thousand pounds and worth it.

A very definite stir could be noted throughout the Sotheby galleries when van Gogh's "Les Usines à Clichy" came up. Everybody was excited except possibly the auctioneer, who asked in a matter-of-fact tone if anybody wanted to give him a starter of five thousand pounds. The same picture had been sold previously in Germany for eighteen hundred pounds. This had those in the audience who knew about it sitting on the edge of their chairs. The auctioneer received his five thousand in a hurry, and after that the bidding went leaping up at a thousand pounds to the bid until it touched thirty-one thousand, the highest bid of the day. It went to Knoedler's.

Knoedler's also paid a fancy price for the famous "Head of an Angel" which van Gogh had painted—apparently just for practice—from an engraving attributed to Rembrandt. Van Gogh himself had never been able to sell it, but this time it went to Knoedler's for twenty-six thousand pounds. And the sale went on through fifty-six items ending finally with a pencil sketch of a carpenter on his way home from work. This went to Hallsborough for two thousand three hundred pounds, bringing the total for the day to three hundred twenty-six thousand, five hundred twenty pounds.

It was a truly magnificent collection of modern paintings—

the work of a lifetime. Not one of the great Impressionists was missing. How many of the paintings will find their way back to America only time will tell. But Sotheby's can always be proud of the fact that when the trend finally turned it came to the rostrum of the oldest of the art-dealing auction houses in all of Britain.

CHAPTER SIXTEEN

CHRISTIE'S

ANOTHER OF THE FAMOUS LONDON AUCTION HOUSES DATING back to the early days still goes by the name of Christie's though there is no longer a Christie in it. In a location on Pall Mall, it was started in 1763 by one James Christie after an apprentice-ship as well as a partnership with one Annesley, a highly re-garded auctioneer of the period. Unlike the Stevens old curi-osity shop, which after starting a bit highbrow as a bookshop soon developed into an auction shop of miscellaneous items, the Christie concern started with the red flag and bell of the ordinary odds and ends auctioneer, and later on went high-brow, dealing exclusively in books and objects of art and beauty, paintings, jewelry, and all the finer things of life.

Christie's first catalogue, dated December 6, 1766, deals largely with commonplace household furnishings, equipment, and effects. Among the articles enumerated are:

Two Nankeen chamber-pots,
Pair of sheets and two pillow-rigs,
Four flatirons, a footman (dumb-waiter), gridiron trivet,
2 brass candlesticks, snuffers, hanging iron, etc.

There was also a lady's sedan chair, and a Chelsea tea service. Wine, too, figures in the collection, and at most attractive prices. From the first he handled an occasional chromo such as a moonlight by Cuyp, which was on the order of an early American masterpiece called "What Are the Wild Waves Saying?" This first catalogue mentions some damaged bronzes "finely repaired by the ingenious Mr. Robiliac."

But these were only incidental, and for some years Christie's was just another ordinary auction room selling the secondhand things that happened to come along in the ordinary run of business. It was not until art collections had started to come his way that he really began to concentrate on the fine and artistic things of life.

He was tall, good-looking, well mannered, and in addition was known to be scrupulously honest, and furthermore he was one of the most urbane, fluent, and witty of the auctioneers of his time. Then too, he was on intimate terms with many of the most distinguished artists of the period which produced such memorable figures as Joshua Reynolds, Garrick, Sheridan, and Gainsborough, who painted a charming portrait of him to be hung in the "Great Room" where the auctions were held.

During the French Revolution there was a steady stream of paintings and other works of art flowing to England because of the confused and warlike conditions prevailing on the Continent. Much of this went to Christie's, which was not long in becoming somewhat famous for its sales of rare and valuable pictures, splendid period furniture, rare jewels, and costly objects of art from the most unimpeachable sources and distinguished collectors.

Probably the most famous collection of pictures to come to England near the end of the eighteenth century was that of the Duke of Orleans, and it contained some of the world's finest pictures by such famous artists Titian, Rembrandt, Raphael, and Velasquez, including the noted "Leda" by Corregio which, with other nudes, was destroyed by order of the Duke's weak-minded son, a religious fanatic greatly influenced by bigoted priests who thought that the beauty of the female form divine could be deprived of its charm by destruction of the painted likeness.

While the urge to collect is one of the oldest and strongest instincts of mankind, as well as the most diversified, it frequently leads to only one place—the auction room. From there a collection may be broken up and scattered into other collections, which after a little time may share the same fate. Should it fall into the hands of a museum, it is still not safe from destruction, for museums are constantly sending surplus articles to the auction room for sale. Otherwise they would be over-whelmed with mediocre talent, some of which is almost certain to slip into the most distinguished collections.

Once James Christie had enjoyed the pleasure and profit of selling a real art collection at auction he swept the pots, pans, and flatirons out of his somewhat commonplace establishment and turned the place into a real auction gallery. With the help of Joshua Reynolds, Gainsborough, and other influential friends, he surrounded himself with artists and collectors and made the premises into a regular hangout where persons of artistic tastes could congregate for friendly gossip and palaver.

The truth is that James Christie, though artistic and highly intelligent, realized that he was not a full-fledged connoisseur, and when in doubt about some work of art he would call on Reynolds and Gainsborough for advice. But Gainsborough died in the late eighties, and Reynolds only four years later.

It so happened that Sir Joshua was not only a famous painter but a noted collector as well; and although some years elapsed before his collection was put on the market, it was naturally brought to Christie's for disposition, whereupon the company was soon involved in one of the most exciting controversies in the history of the firm.

On the day of the sale the street in front of the auction gallery was thronged with carriages and excited crowds of fashionable people. In commenting on the occasion, one of the newspapers remarked, "Such a sensation has never before been experienced in the picture world of London."

A stranger passing Christie's might have thought that some great lady was giving a reception, which indeed was the case. But the great lady had been in her grave, lo! these many years, and it was her portrait, alleged to have been painted by Gainsborough, that was causing all the sensation. Throughout her lifetime the Duchess of Devonshire, one of the great beauties of her day, was talked about; and here, despite all the years that had elapsed since her passing, she was on the tip of everybody's tongue. This time it was not her wit or her beauty but her authenticity that was in doubt.

Was this the famous Gainsborough original, or had Sir Joshua been the victim of a gigantic fraud and deception?

For weeks before the sale the papers had been full of letters and articles raising serious doubts as to the genuineness of the portrait. Some of the distinguished Royal Academicians were convinced that it was *the* Gainsborough—and in his best manner. Others, while admitting that the portrait was charming, were equally certain that it was not the work of Gainsborough. Aside from the experts and critics, people generally had accepted it with enthusiasm, and when the canvas was finally placed on the auction room easel there was a thunder of applause.

Bidding was started at a thousand pounds. In the tense silence of the opening came a bid from Agnew, one of the more daring of the local dealers. He raised the bid to five thousand, which was quickly followed with a flurry of bids which ran up to thirty thousand. Then came a pause as if the bidders had run out of breath. This was getting into the big money for those days and people were giving each other questing sidelong

glances. Was this going to be the end? Agnew answered the
question for them. He raised the bid to thirty-five thousand.
Another flurry of bids followed, with Agnew holding at fifty
thousand.

At the big picture sales in England the auctioneers are exceedingly well mannered. There is no chanting, no yipping,
yapping, or bellowing. Mr. Wood, the auctioneer, glanced over
the auditorium. "Is there anyone else?" he asked quietly, "or
are you all done?"

When there was no answer, the white ivory gavel came
down decisively. Mr. Wood's lips moved but nobody could
hear what he said because of the great outburst of cheering and
applause. It was as if the favorite had won the Derby or a
popular team had captured the cup at a cricket match. Staid
Englishmen slapped strangers on the back or embraced people
they had never seen before. After the furor had subsided Mr.
Wood announced that the picture had been sold to Mr. Agnew
for fifty thousand pounds, and went on to explain that the price
was the highest sum ever bid at Christie's for a single picture.

And the Duchess, as was her way, managed to keep in the
spotlight for Mr. Agnew placed the picture on exhibition in his
show window where she instantly became the toast of the
town. But alas, one night a thief entered the place, cut her
portrait out of the frame, and succeeded in getting away with
it. Not until seventeen years later was it found in a little shop
in Chicago and returned to the owner.

But America, after all, was to be the permanent home of
the Duchess, for the portrait was bought by J. Pierpont Morgan
for 175,000 good American dollars and now hangs at the Metropolitan Museum in New York.

Many crowned heads have contributed to the fame of
Christie's, probably the earliest being Mary, Queen of Scots,
when in 1767 a "Signum of the Holy Ghost" set with diamonds,
emeralds, rubies and other precious stones came into Christie's

to be put up for sale. It had been given by the Queen to a lady-in-waiting shortly before her Majesty was beheaded. It was well authenticated, having remained in the family of the donee continuously until brought to Christie's for sale. But like many of the gems of royalty the Signum was supposed to carry a curse, and despite the high market value of the jewels it contained, it brought only twelve guineas, the equivalent of about sixty dollars at the time.

About a century and a half later Christie's had the honor of selling the betrothal cup presented to the Scottish Queen by her bridegroom, Dauphin François II, in 1558. By this time the curse on the ill-fated queen's relics seems to have been laid, for the holy cup, a Limoges *tazza*, fetched over seventeen hundred pounds.

Another fabulous relic of the hapless queen was the curious "Cruckstone Dollar" which was sold at the Hamilton Place sale in 1882. It was struck upon her marriage with Lord Henry Stewart and set in a frame of wood cut from the yew tree under which he is reputed to have courted her. Carved on the frame was the following verse:

"When Harie met Marie under this yew tree,
What Harie did to Marie I'll no tell to thee."

Christie's could have made a fair living out of the items which came to the firm connected with Horatio, Lord Nelson, and his friend Lady Hamilton. The greater part of it came through milady in the form of letters, pictures, gifts, and trinkets which came dribbling in for years after Nelson's death. Indeed, as late as 1914 a valuable and revealing collection of letters he had written to her between 1785 and 1800 was sold at Christie's. Some of them gave graphic details of his operations in and around Corsica and the besieged cities of Bastia and Calvi, and

there was also his account of the battle of St. Vincent and
various other engagements.

He was so madly in love with the beautiful woman that he
used little discretion about some of the things he wrote to her.
She, on the other hand, preserved every scrap of paper she
received from him, realizing no doubt that they would become
more and more valuable with the passage of time. In fact, she
was so discreet about the Corsican letters that Nelson's early
biographers were unaware of their existence when they were
writing of his career.

One of the most important of the Nelson letters came to
Christie's as late as 1905. It was a signed memorandum in his
own handwriting giving the plan for the attack at Trafalgar
precisely as it was subsequently carried out. It brought under
the hammer the handsome sum of thirty-six hundred pounds.
In another letter to Lady Hamilton, sold as late as 1924 though
dated in 1801, he implored her not to let the Prince of Wales
enter her door. Only a man who has been in love with "another
woman" will appreciate this inane appeal.

Of all Romney's fascinating portraits of Lady Hamilton
which have passed under the Christie hammer, the most charming is that in which she is shown as a Bacchante leading—of all
things—a goat. Could there have been some hidden innuendo
here?

Though the Christie firm has been through half a dozen or
more changes of title and is now officially designated as Christie, Manson and Woods, the last actual connection of a Christie
with the establishment ceased when James H. B. Christie, son
of George Henry Christie, retired in 1889 to lead the life of
a country gentleman.

During the years 1928-1929, the Christie firm reached its
high-water mark with a turnover in excess of two million
pounds. One sale followed another in quick succession with

buyers from all parts of the world willing to pay the most fantastic prices. Perhaps the greatest event at Christie's between the two wars was the sale of the Sir George Holford collection. It was indeed an exciting sale. When the announcement appeared in the papers there was a mad rush for seats, but so much of the space had already been allotted to dealers who had come to London from afar expressly for the sale that not more than two hundred nonprofessionals succeeded in obtaining admission.

The big moment came when Mr. Lance Hannen, perhaps the most imperturbable man in the Christie organization, mounted the rostrum in what was distinctly a first-night atmosphere. He paused for a moment as a superb little Rembrandt was placed on the easel, then said in a low voice as if he might have been opening an ordinary sale on a foggy night with the seats only half filled:

"Lot One. How much for this?"

The first bid came from Mr. Sabin. It was two thousand guineas. Then the dam burst and bids came pouring in from every side. The Rembrandt went to Colnagi for ten thousand guineas. This and three other Rembrandts brought a total of 148,000 guineas. Excitement in the crowded room was intense. One could almost hear the panting of people. The first days intake was over 364,000 pounds. The second day brought the total to nearly half a milion. New records were made not only by the Old Masters—for which American bidders seemed willing to pay almost any price, but the Modernists, too, were coming into their own. Manet, Renoir, Sisley, Pissaro, and a dozen of their contemporaries were bringing unheard-of figures.

Although the sale was a magnificent success it was, in a way, like the kiss of death, for the great American slump of 1929 was just around the corner, and when the crash came the reverberations could be felt in every corner of the globe. And for the next decade the civilized world was on the verge of bankruptcy or worse.

In September, 1938, a gentleman with an umbrella made "peace in our time," and almost before we realized what was going on all the world except the American continent was aflame with war. It was no time for dealing in the art treasures of the world; rather it was a time for hiding them away from the ruthless invader, the destroyer, the thief.

However, finding a safe refuge for the vast amount of treasure in the Christie establishment alone had not yet been fully accomplished when on April 16, 1941, the Luftwaffe found its mark with a blockbuster and made a direct hit on Christie's famous King Street rooms to which the firm had moved in 1885.

When the smoke and dust had cleared away, nothing was left standing of the noble building but the portico and a fragment of crumbled wall while the interior was no more than a bed of coals. The generous loan of a building by Lord Derby enabled the firm to continue what business there was, with a minimum of interruption. But not until the 25th of April was it possible for Sir Alex and his staff to examine the vaults and strong rooms which had been buried under the smouldering rubble. Wreckers were forced to cut their way in with acetyline torches. They found only one of the safes completely unharmed, and fortunately it was the one containing the magnificent and unreplaceable collection of jewels which had been donated for the great Red Cross sale.

It so happened that there were no paintings of great value in the house at the time of the bombing and the contents of the other strongboxes were only slightly damaged, so the unique collection of auction catalogues dating from 1766 suffered no injury except slight damage from water.

The firm remained in the Lord Derby building for six years,

and when that was sold there was a brief interval in the Earl
Spencer house, after which they moved into their new home
on the old King Street site with all its memories and traditions
from which they had been blitzed by the cohorts of a crazy
house painter, at which location the saying had originated that
to have come under the hammer at Christie's is a guarantee of
value either intrinsic or historic.

CHAPTER SEVENTEEN

STEVENS'

THE THIRD OLDEST OF THE FAMOUS AUCTION ROOMS IN ENGLAND was started by Samuel Paterson at 38 King Street, Covent Garden, in 1776 while the conflict known as the Revolutionary War was being fought in the American Colonies. Being a well-known bibliographer, Mr. Paterson dealt principally with books, manuscripts, and prints at the beginning of his auctioneering career, cataloguing and selling many valuable collections. In one of these, papers containing some important documents by Julius Caesar were about to be sold as wastepaper to a cheesemonger when Paterson discovered the error and rescued them. Their subsequent sale by auction brought three hundred and fifty-six pounds, worth at that time some seventeen hundred of our dollars.

Paterson initiated the practice of selling books in lots, starting the bidding at sixpence, with threepenny advances until five shillings had been reached, whereupon the bidding proceeded at no less than sixpence. From these figures it will be seen that Paterson had no high-flown ideas of becoming rich, but he would have been richer if he had not been so fond of reading his own books and chatting with the bookish clan who soon made a gathering place of 38 King. Dr. Johnson was a frequent caller and hanger-on there, and of course Boswell was around with his perpetual listening-ear. Garrick, a diligent collector of theatrical material, was in and out almost daily, while Gough, editor of *Camden's Britannia*, in top boots, carrying a whip, and looking very much the part of John Bull, would occasionally drop in. Dr. Lort, chaplain to the Duke of Devonshire, in thick woolen stockings and a "Busby" wig, was often in the place as well as Mr. Pitt and Horace Walpole, both of whom were confirmed collectors.

A few years before his death Mr. Paterson was succeeded by Messrs. King, Collins and Chapman. Soon Collins withdrew and the concern went on under the name and style of Chapman & King; by 1796 Chapman had withdrawn and the firm continued as King & Son. Secondhand books were cheap at the time, but one lot of ancient poems containing Chaucer's "Troylus and Cresyde" and "Temple of Glass," printed by Wynkyn de Worde, went for twenty-six pounds. Another interesting lot consisted of a first (1667), a second (1668), and a third, (1669) edition of *Paradise Lost*, which were bid in at eleven shillings each, the catalogue stating that the different title pages were used "to force the sale of that matchless poem."

In 1806 a first edition of *A Midsummer Night's Dream* went under the hammer for three pounds three shillings; and several other first editions of separate plays by the Bard fetched no more than five to seven pounds. That same day Dr. Burney, who was a frequent visitor at the rooms, bid in a book simply because of its interesting title which was:

> "Rules to get Children with Handsome Faces,
> so that their children may not have such
> Strange, Prodigious, Ill-boding Faces as their
> Fathers, 1642."

That worthy volume went for only seven shillings sixpence, whereas a book on Purgatorye telling "where and what the place is, what Paynes that be therein, and where soules do abyde till they be purged of Synne; and for what synes a Soul goeth to Hell, and of the help Soules may have of theyr Frends on lyve," a splendid opus in verse, black letter with a wood cut, went for seventeen pounds, which was after all a small price for getting the low-down on Purgatorye.

There was a big change in the atmosphere of 38 King Street when the management abandoned the policy of books exclusively and announced an important sale of a collection of shells gathered by one William Webber. The old conservative customers shook their heads dubiously over this radical change of policy, but on the day of the sale the conchologists crowded the rooms and bid so enthusiastically that other conchological sales quickly followed and it was not long before the mammoth collection of William Broadrip of Bristol opened a sale which lasted for five consecutive days.

The auctioning of mineral collections was started at about this same period. It went along rather indifferently for a while until a stranger came along one day and asked to be allowed to unpack his collection during one of the Friday sales. Put on sale it fetched over one thousand pounds and sold a number of specimens that went directly to the British Museum. From that time on the sale of minerals was one of the regular lines at 38 King Street for many years.

Books receded ever further into the background when the first collection of insects came in at the door. It was not long before the noted collection of John Francillon was put on sale for an auction that ran nine days and at which every naturalist of note was to be seen. A single beetle, *Prionus giganteus* (sex undetermined) fetched a record price of more than five pounds. A butterfly, *Papilio homerus* went for six pounds, and a *Phasma*, described as a giant insect from New Holland, went for one pound two.

Among other notable events at this time were the sales of Leverian and London Museums. The Leverian was a remarkable

collection of ethnological interest which filled sixteen rooms in
Leicester House on Leicester Square. The selling of this collection under the hammer lasted sixteen days without intermission,
"except Sundays and the King's birthday."

Wide interest was aroused by the specimens collected by
Captain Cook on his three voyages of discovery. These brought
spirited bidding, some of the articles being bought for museums
not only in Britain, but on the Continent as well.

From time to time paintings by one of the Old Masters came
into the auction rooms for sale—such names as Rembrandt,
Brueghel, Reynolds, and Rubens were sometimes to be heard.
Paintings by Benjamin West before he had attained fame were
frequently sold there for modest prices; his "Expulsion of Adam
and Eve" bringing only twenty-four pounds, and "Peter's First
Sermon" going under the hammer at thirty pounds. His "Venus
Attired by the Graces" reached a low of seventeen pounds and
a fraction.

J. C. Stevens had come into the firm in the 1820's, and by
1834 his name was on the door as sole proprietor; from that time
on the King Street rooms continued in the control of the Stevens
family, passing from father to son until the institution was well
past the century mark.

J. C. was a born collector, having made a collection of cherry
pits when only a lad. Whether this collection was ever shown
in the auction rooms does not appear. But he had quite a liking
for insects and had sold several well-known collections before
the famous Haworth bugs had come into his auction rooms. It
had been half a century in the making and contained some forty
thousand specimens, the sale of which occupied eleven entire
days and attracted every bug man of note in the British Isles
and many from the Continent.

For the first six days *Coleoptera*, *Orthoptera*, and *Strepsistera*
occupied the rostrum, and then gave way to *Lepidoptera* for
the next five days. While the proceeds of the sale, somewhat

over twenty-five hundred dollars in American money, is no startling amount, it is quite a bit to pay for insects most of which are regarded as pests by everybody and everything except the collectors and the birds. And speaking of birds, Mr. Stevens soon built a thriving business with all kinds of birds and their eggs. His success with the Great Auk alone would no doubt have made him famous with the collectors, for he became known as the "Auk King" and was so proud of this title that he adopted it as his telegraphic address, and *"Auks, London"* became as widely known among ornithologists as *"Ford, Detroit"* is among motorists. The auk was exterminated by greedy human beings who found that the bird was good to eat and easy to catch, and like the extinct passenger pigeon had no adequate means of defense, being unable to fly.

Before the great slaughter, auks' eggs could have been obtained by the thousand, for the birds were teeming on their breeding grounds; but when in 1853, after they were gone, Mr. Stevens took a census of the known eggs, he found in the hands of collectors only seventy-five all told.

Twenty-five of these had found their way to the King Street rooms and were sold there, several of them changing hands a number of times at prices ranging from twenty pounds to three hundred and thirty. Forty-four of the recorded eggs were in Great Britain, seven in France, five in Germany, two in Holland, fourteen in the United States, and one each in Denmark, Portugal, and Switzerland. The highest price the auction room ever received for one was three hundred and thirty pounds, and the last one sold at the Stevens auction rooms went under the hammer in 1900.

The egg of the *Aepyornis maximus*, an extinct bird of Madagascar, is much larger than the egg of the auk, which is about the size of a man's fist; the egg-shell of the *Aepyornis*, however, will hold some two gallons of fluid or the equivalent of one hundred and thirty-five hen's eggs. Only twenty eggs of this giant bird exist, but they are far less valuable than those of the auk, for as Mr. Stevens explains, "It has never been a British bird."

Mr. Stevens next went in for ethnological sales, his interest having been aroused by the collection of an Egyptian officer which had been brought to his auction rooms. The specimens consisted largely of scarabs, beads, statues of a strange lion-headed deity, and a quantity of coins. These Egyptian articles sold so readily that Mr. Stevens decided to take a flyer in mummies, four of which were placed on exhibition at the auction rooms. The owner insisted that one of the four was all that remained of Queen Nefertari, wife of Rameses II. But the public was skeptical. What would a queen be doing in a mummy without a case? The owner explained that the sand had shifted away and uncovered the case which had been rotted away by the elements. And when the skeptics were still doubtful, he unwrapped the lower part of a queenly leg and cut into the member far enough to prove that a body was really there. With this reassurance the queen was placed on sale and brought twelve pounds.

The newspaper publicity given to the queen brought crowds to the next sale, and although the other three mummies were without cases or hieroglyphics they sold as a lot for seventy-five guineas. Thereupon Mr. Stevens ordered more mummies from Egypt and also from Peru and Ecuador and established quite a lively trade in the remains of those who had died many centuries before.

Hearing of this, an army man who had spent some time in Africa brought to the auction rooms four portmanteaux containing his collection of shrunken heads purchased from the natives. He had been keeping them in his bedroom for company at night. He reported that he had found them a great comfort and explained that whenever he had a wakeful night it was his practice to get up out of bed and comb the hair of a few of the

Maoris, which he found soothing and relaxing. Other tenants in the building told a different story about moans and groans and rattling chains beginning at exactly the midnight hour, and threatened to move out unless the shrunken heads were disposed of. Put up for sale, the army officer's collection brought under the hammer from twenty to forty pounds a head.

For the first half century of its existence only inanimate objects had been dealt with at this old curiosity shop on King Street. Then Mr. Stevens let down the bars for Lord Derby's menagerie and aviary. Milord's menagerie consisted of deer, antelopes, goats, sheep, llamas, rodents, lemurs, armadillos, and a duckbill platypus. Among the birds were falcons, vultures, owls, kingfishers, parrots, and many rare songbirds. The gnus should also be mentioned, the elands, and a pair of wapiti which sold for one hundred and five pounds. A Brahman bull went for fifty pounds while a yak brought one hundred and a quagga, surprisingly enough, brought fifty.

A still larger menagerie followed when the animals of the Surrey Zoological Gardens went under the hammer. The scale of prices brought is not without interest. A lioness was sold for one hundred and fifty pounds whereas her husband brought two hundred and twenty-five. An elephant brought three hundred and thirty-six pounds, and a giraffe three hundred. Camels seldom went for more than sixty pounds, and a two-horned rhinoceros could be had for eight-two. A black bok was bid up to forty-six, and a koodoo brought only five pounds.

Henry Stevens was only a child when he heard his father tell how Mr. Skinner had come to him with a few petals of orchid asking what he could do with such frail and beautiful flowers. There was practically no sale for them at the time, but as they began to be seen in the market people started to buy them and almost immediately developed a desire to grow them. After a slow start they came suddenly into public favor and soon were all the rage.

Mr. Stevens was in on the ground floor for he was already raising and selling orchids when they were still new to the public; and soon after the craze had become well started he set aside Thursday of each week as Orchid Day. The next step was the sending of orchid hunters to the tropical jungles of the world in quest of new varieties. Mr. Skinner, one of the most tireless of the collectors who brought their discoveries to the King Street Auctions, took up a long residence in Guatamala searching the jungles as if under the spell of the magical flower.

The orchid story reads like a fairy tale. A little bloom that sold for three or four shillings one year would come back the next with plants and blossoms which went under the hammer at one hundred and seventy-three pounds. It was almost like a gold strike or an oil gusher, and soon everybody was doing it.

An American syndicate paid twelve thousand pounds for only part of a collection, and the plants left over brought another twelve thousand pounds under the hammer. There came a time, however, when the tide began to ebb. The sale of orchids had become more or less standardized and the rage as such was coming to an end. Not that the cult of the orchid lover has entirely ended or ever will so long as man's love of beauty continues to exist.

The English are predominantly relic lovers and, located in London surrounded by members of the Royal family the auction rooms were naturally the haven for royal relics. What is a souvenir or relic to one may be junk or rubbish to another, and it must sometimes have been difficult at all the great auction galleries to know whether to put an article on sale or to drop it into the ash barrel.

But alas, Mr. Stevens is gone. His old King Street auction house is also gone—blown off the face of the earth by a block-buster in World War II, and the place where the building once stood is now occupied by a greengrocer.

CHAPTER EIGHTEEN

FREAK AUCTIONS

THOUGH AUCTIONS IN THIS COUNTRY HAVE BECOME THOROUGHLY standardized, though they operate under the same rules and regulations, make the same ballyhoo, and use the same terms, though they are all conducted for the same purpose—selling things, largely secondhand—they occasionally turn up a delectable freak. Take the "Believe It or Not!" auction staged at the Plaza Galleries in New York by Ripley's estate a few years ago. This vendue was not only conducted for the sale of freaks, but it was largely attended by freaks, many of whom had come quite obviously to find out whether they *could* believe it or not. Even the catalogue was a freak, for it contained among other nugatory information the statement that Mr. Ripley, who ordinarily received more than a million letters a year, had traveled six hundred thousand miles in quest of freaks for his syndicated series.

Whether this was more or less mileage than that traveled by Mr. Phineas T. Barnum in his search for oddities for his museum and side show is neither here nor there. The two collectors were working at cross purposes. Mr. Barnum wanted his audiences to love Mr. and Mrs. Tom Thumb and the rest of his so-called freaks, Jennie Lind, and Jumbo, while Ripley merely wanted to shock and amaze his audience.

As he gathered his freaks Ripley was also collecting furniture and objects of art for his several homes and his well-named Chinese houseboat or junk; but he knew little about either art or furniture, and it is often difficult to tell the freaks from the furnishings. It was a motley and heterogeneous collection of freaks there at the Plaza Galleries when the doors were thrown open to the public. But it was also a motley and heterogeneous public which crowded in to see and perhaps to bid on it. Most of them had come out of curiosity, but there must have been some who came for business, since the auction lasted three days, and believe it or not, the receipts totaled nearly $90,000.

Ripley must have visited China, or at least Chinatown, many times for there was a Mongolian preponderance to his collection; and he had acquired, as collectors of the oriental always seem to acquire, several of those large stone pieces such as used to be seen in Gump's at San Francisco, though one could never tell whether they were meant for gravestones, hecates, garden seats or what-not. These monumental pieces were bought mostly by dealers though it was difficult to move them in and out without a derrick.

He must also have visited the Pacific Northwest, for he had collected three totem poles, objects heretofore regarded as unsalable by merchants and especially by auctioneers. These, however, must have broken the hex, for they went for $760. It would be interesting to know where they are today.

The auction gallery was packed and from the beginning the bidding was sprightly. And who should be seen there among the crowd but Cardinal Spellman, who had quite obviously come to bid on a large plaster statuette of the good St. Patrick. The Cardinal entered the contest early and stayed with it up to $40 where he dropped out. As it turned out, he never had a chance, for the bidding went gaily on up to $200 where it was struck down to a red-headed gentleman named John Arthur

who had already bought the world rights to the Ripley newspaper "feature," along with a vast quantity of freakish furnishings from the various Ripley domiciles and was planning to
make "Believe It or Not" into a real world-wide comic strip,
though it was already well on its way. Mr. Arthur also bought
the Ripley houseboat which he was considering making into a
floating museum, though that project seems to have been lost
sight of.

Another active bidder at the auction was Harry Richman,
an old Broadway song and dance man, who bought a collection
of huge tankards, one fashioned from an elephant tusk. These
were intended for his Reno ranch, a place where guests no doubt
appreciated a lusty draught. He put up a gallant battle for a
drinking vessel—one could hardly call it a stein—fashioned from
a walrus tusk, and again it was John Arthur who beat off a rival
bidder and carried away the prize.

Richman was naturally disappointed, but he was soon battling
with better success, for a huge Japanese sword, and he also
acquired a collection of canes, twenty-five of them, which will
come in handy if he ever returns to the song-and-dance business. However, Harry had a slight mishap when he undertook
to wave his hand to an acquaintance across the room, for the
auctioneer, mistaking the motion for a bid, struck down to him
an oriental bedspread for $40. And gentleman that he is, Harry
accepted it and paid for it, not without a colloquy, however.

Among the macabre items were several shrunken human
heads which were bid on as gaily as if they were not portions of
dead human beings. There were a number of primitive masks, a
six-armed Vishnu, a snarling ceramic canine, and a General Electric sun lamp with a self-timer. Great interest was evinced by
the women present in item No. 948 which was a reducing roller
made by the Chinese by stringing an arrangement of colored
glass balls with which to roll off hips, tummies, and thighs. They

picked up the apparatus, examined it with care, inquiring exactly how it was used, and several asked in an undertone, "But does it really work?"

A pair of newly-weds who were looking for some real originality in the furnishings for their new home hesitated for some time between an enormous wooden statue of an aborigine goddess of good luck and a lacquered opium bed which would certainly have opened the eyes of their homefolk when told what it was. But they finally decided on the goddess, probably because they were fearful that people might get the idea they were dope fiends, and they had to go up above $200 to get it.

By the end of the third day every last thing had gone under the hammer, even a rather horrible brass head, some tribal weapons, a deep-sea diver's knife, some framed butterflies, and a Chinese rug marked in the catalogue "as is"—and it most certainly *was*.

One can count on Paris to double almost any kind of freak that can be imagined. Speak of a freak auction and Paris immediately comes up with two kinds not to be found anywhere else on earth. She has an outdoor auction which is constantly in session, that is, it meets once every twenty-four hours, though never twice consecutively in the same place. Its usual meeting place is in the sewers, or during the hot weather in some dark alley, but it invariably meets under cover of darkness. It is an organization of crooks, criminals, thieves, pickpockets, muggers, and holdup men, to say nothing of highway robbers.

Their purpose is to get together while the stolen goods are still "hot," and pass them into the hands of somebody else who cannot possibly be under suspicion, preferably somebody who has an airtight alibi covering the exact period of the theft. The thief exhibits the goods, explains the alibi needed, and calls for bids. If the goods are desirable the bidding may be lively. But if they happen to be dubious, of secondary value, or hard to dispose of there may be offers of a swap which will get both parties off the hook by a mutual exchange.

They are all cutthroats and hardened criminals, and for an honest man, an innocent man, to stumble into one of their auctions would be a real tragedy, for they would either murder him on the spot or if they happened to be in a tender mood they might do no worse than to put out his eyes and possibly cut off an ear or two.

There is nothing criminal about the little shops along the Right Bank though they will cheat you if they possibly can. You must bargain for anything that you get there; they never expect to sell at their asking price, but if you can't agree after a little palaver they will offer to sell it by auction and will immediately begin with their auctioneers' cry, stopping pedestrians, dragging in bystanders, and even calling taxicab drivers down from their stands. Of course it is impossible to tell who are their stooges, and if you go on with it you are sure to lose out. However, if you know your art goods you can often pick up a valuable etching or painting—stolen as like as not, but how can you tell? And they're likely to sell it cheaper if they think the police are going to come along and pick it up. Sometimes they soil new pictures to make them look like Old Masters. And again the one you are looking at may *be* an Old Master—you never can tell.

But while these little kiosks are fun, they are not to be compared with the Hotel Drouot, which is not a hotel at all, but which claims to be the world's largest collection of permanent auctions. It covers five entire city blocks lying to the east of the Opera—at least it did when I last saw it. At that time it had been there over a hundred years, and unless there's been another war that I haven't heard of you'll find it right there today. It's in the neighborhood of the American Express Company where you naturally go to cash your checks, so you'll have some ready money in your pocket if there's anything you want to buy.

Let me assure you that you can find anything you can possibly want there if you have patience enough to keep on hunting. You may have to go back a number of times, but eventually it will turn up.

You may happen upon a Whistler etching—one that he dropped on the floor and possibly stepped on. I saw one that had been bought in Drouot for $5 on which the heel-mark was plainly apparent. It was on display in a San Francisco shop and was priced at $1,000, the heel-mark giving it an added distinction. The story was that it was rescued by a charwoman and sold for a shilling or two to a dustman who knew enough to get it out of the country. This was while Whistler was living in England. It found its way to the Hotel Drouot and an American tourist bid it in. No discriminating collector would have had it at any price; but in California—who knows?

Word about this fascinating auction mart reaches the tourist in Paris before he has had time to unpack his bag, and if he is the usual American bargain hunter it is likely to be the first place to which he goes. The most fabulous things happen to the Americans who go there. One woman, while looking for some jet buttons which were in style at the time, came home with a picture she was sure was an Old Master. It was soiled and grimy, had a slight tear in one corner, and the frame was all but broken away. Her opening bid of 100 francs bought it and she felt sure that she had found an Old Master until her husband saw it. He said it had all the earmarks of a fake and almost persuaded her to throw it away, but she finally insisted on taking it to America. There after she had spent another $25 to have it cleaned she found that she had an early Titian worth several thousand dollars.

The next time she visited the Hotel Drouot she saw a collection of autographs including those of Alexander Hamilton, Voltaire, Marie Antoinette, David Lloyd George, and Victor Hugo. They were not very expensive, but remembering her husband's conniption over the painting, she passed them by. This time he scolded because she had not bought them, but when she went back the next day they were gone. Bid in by another American, the man said.

Hotel Drouot is always crowded with tourists from the ends of the earth; but of them all the Americans are the biggest suckers. They are the ones who buy the clocks without works, the unfinished Old Masters on which the paint is hardly dry, the Napoleon snuffboxes which are carefully dented and oxidized before being put on display. The clerk tells you genially that they've had everything on sale there except the Eiffel Tower, and they're expecting that any day; and you tell him that if they ever do get it one of the Americans who have already bought the Brooklyn Bridge will be right there to bid on it.

Drouot is a noisy and confusing place with twenty or more auctions going on at once; but you do get some wonderful bargains there though they all are bought with a neat little *caveat emptor* which is printed on the sale slip and painted on the walls of the buildings to the effect that "No reclamation will be admitted once the adjudication has been pronounced." In other words there is no comeback after the hammer has fallen.

Of all the freak auctions, the murder and suicide sales are among the best attended and most eagerly contested. Why people, especially women, should jam themselves into a house or an auction room to scramble for the property of some poor unfortunate who has met with a violent death is almost beyond comprehension. Of course the psychiatrists have a glib explanation for it, but it is mostly made up of words which mean little to any except the occult.

I have inquired about this of a number of auctioneers and the answer has always been the same. Nothing like it to bring out a crowd—mostly women dead-set on buying some souvenir that has belonged to the victim. The more sensational the crime the better the sale.

There was a famous case in Germantown, Pennsylvania, where a young boy asked his grandmother for a nickel, and when she refused he flew into a rage and bashed her brains out with a baseball bat—his favorite bat. The auction of her worldly goods brought out a crowd of more than five thousand persons though her personal effects were not worth much over two thousand dollars. But this case seemed to have all the color demanded by such an event—it was bloody, sensational, horrible, a child criminal, an atrocious murder, and more impressive than all else, a bloody weapon.

The church auction was never intended as an institution dealing in freaks. It was undoubtedly started as a business venture intended to make money for a worthy cause without any initial investment. Wall Street would tell you that such a thing is impossible, and your lawyer would probably advise you that if you should try it you would no doubt land in jail. But wherever you see a country church, the chances are about ten to one that you are looking at an institution which at least once a year puts on a successful auction without spending a nickel for the merchandise that goes under the hammer.

Some of them are called rummage sales, some are White Elephants, and others stylishly call themselves church vendues. But they all make money, every penny of which is used for religious purposes such as keeping a carpet on the church floor and a parson in the pulpit. And the churchgoers have a gift for digging up and donating to the sale rare and unusual objects that are seldom seen anywhere except at a church auction, many of which are eligible to be included in a collection of freaks.

Where else would you find a "betty lamp" which was one of the earliest appliances to be used in the days when whale oil first supplanted the candle? Can you think of another place where you would expect to find a "tappit hen" with two chicks which turns out to be a beautiful quart-size, flat-top pewter tankard with matching replicas in a pint and half-pint size? These were found at a church auction in Maine. And it was also at a church auction that a genuine Dr. Syntax soup tureen was discovered which threw the congregation into ecstasies when it turned out to be a great rarity and brought $300 under the hammer. At a New Jersey church auction a "trussing coffer" brought $200 and two "dwarf stall" chairs sold for almost as much, while a Virginia congregation was thrilled over a clock with spandrils, and at an auction at an upstate church in New York a freakish "sliding-stick" candleholder came to light equipped with an arrangement by which the candle could be made to slide up as fast as it burned down.

Not long ago I saw at a church auction in Massachusetts a curious object about the size of a stovepipe section three feet long with large holes cut in the sides and a chain at one end by which it could be hung in the flue of a chimney to prevent a backdraft from blowing smoke into the room, and also to keep witches from coming down the chimney. There was a time when this might have been a useful appliance to have in a Massachusetts chimney, but I am told that not a single witch has been seen in the Bay State within the last hundred years.

The auctions of the country churches are usually held during the growing season when fruits, potted plants, and vegetables are donated. Large baskets of selected peaches, plums, and apples ordinarily ornament the rostrum and find eager bidders awaiting them. Nearly always these fruit baskets are screened with plastic to prevent sampling, even though the audience is made up largely of church members.

In the truly rural areas lambs, rabbits, poultry, and occasionally a calf will be donated to one of these auctions. Only once have I heard of a hive of bees being on sale at a church auction, and after what happened I doubt if it will be tried again. All went well until the auctioneer, in making a sale, brought down his hammer on the top of the hive with enough force not only to make a loud bang, but to displace the cover of the hive, releasing a stream of angry bees thirsting for the blood of the marauders who had so rudely disturbed their afternoon siesta.

The first attacking wave struck the auctioneer squarely in the face, and flailing with his arms to ward off the attack he upset the hive and not only spilled the honey but released the entire swarm, all of them madder than the proverbial hornet.

Events were moving so fast that only those who were nearest the beehive were aware of what was happening, and when they tried to leave the place as expeditiously as possible, they were obstructed by the crowds of curious people on the outside who were trying to get close enough to the scene of action to find out what was going on.

In the confusion the bees for a time had things their own way, but eventually the situation clarified itself and the victims withdrew to a nearby brook where they knelt in a row along the bank for healing mudpacks, while a professional beekeeper righted the hive and predicted that every last bee would be in it by sunset; and since the auctioneer was nowhere to be found, the auction was unanimously adjourned until the following Saturday.

And in the meantime it was currently remarked around town that it was the first time that anyone had ever been stung at one of the church auctions.

CHAPTER NINETEEN

THE SUPERAUCTION

EVERYBODY LOVED WANAMAKER'S. GOOD OLD WANAMAKER'S. IT wasn't the speediest place on earth, but it was one of the best. You could trust Wanamaker's; it never cheated anybody out of a farthing. It charged plenty, but it surely gave good value. If anything went bad after you bought it Wanamaker's would always make it good. The clerks were a little slow; most of them had been there for a long time and some were getting a bit rickety, but they made few mistakes and never misrepresented their product.

There was a leisurely air about the place. Nobody seemed to be in a hurry, not even the elevators. The operators never hustled you into one as if trying to catch a train, and if you asked one of them a question you received a reply that was not only civil but informative, and sometimes even chatty. After being jostled around in a cut-price shop trying to save a couple of dimes, tired and distraught shoppers would drop into Wanamaker's for a rest.

Here were places where you could sit down, and if a woman wanted to take off her shoes nobody objected. I have often seen weary shoppers, especially in the summertime, sitting there in stocking feet. And once when there was no other place to sit I saw an elderly man with several bundles sitting on a step of the grand staircase wiping his hatband with his handkerchief.

I had a feeling that this would never be allowed and I waited around to see what would happen. Several floorwalkers passed, and if they saw him they paid no attention. But after a while one of them did go up and speak to him, but not in a critical way. He simply asked the old gentleman if he was feeling all right.

The old fellow looked up with a smile. "Just tired, that's all."

At that the floorwalker also smiled. "Most natural thing in the world," he said. "Pretty muggy today." And he went on with his floorwalking. Perhaps you used to get a little tired of those one-line sermons of the Founder which used to appear at the top of the daily advertisement. I did, but I used to look every day to see if it wasn't about time for him to run out of material. It seemed to me from his writings that he didn't want people to get the idea that his store was an ordinary commercial enterprise; but had more of the atmosphere of a Sunday school.

It was a big shock to the public when the original founder died in 1922, but not half the shock it was when in 1955 the announcement was made that the Wanamaker New York store was going out of business. The people of America, especially of New York, couldn't have been any more surprised if Santa Claus had come out with a personal announcement that he was going out of business and there would be no more Christmas.

Rumors began flying all over the place. Some said it was the suburban shopping centers that had driven the store out of business. Others said that the Wanamakers had been losing money for years because they were too stubborn to move uptown. And tales were floating around that the store was going to move to Miami, or to Chicago, or even to Los Angeles.

Not much news came from the store until January 26, when there was an official announcement that the store property had been sold to a syndicate headed by an attorney named David Rapoport; price not mentioned, but the newspapers produced figures of an assessed valuation of $7,375,000 of which $2,157,000 was for the real estate. When asked what was to be done with the building Mr. Rapoport replied that no decision had been made. Conversion to an office building was being considered, and it was just possible that the north building might be rebuilt into an apartment for 1,500 families.

The S. Klein Company of Union Square, always interested in a good remainder, began negotiating for the Wanamaker merchandise. Klein had no desire for the fixtures, but he was willing to make an offer for the dry goods, dress goods, and all the allied lines that could be handled through his Union Square establishment. All the "soft goods," as Klein put it, but not the glassware, crockery, furniture, cutlery, or any of the other "hardware or hard goods."

This was a puzzler for the Wanamaker people. To dispose of all the dry goods in a single transaction was tempting; but what about the rest of the stock? Would there be enough for a really successful auction? While they were thinking about it Klein made a definite offer reported to be $110,000 in cash. After all, money does talk, and it won the argument. Wanamaker accepted and turned over the rest of the merchandise which Klein couldn't handle to the Parke-Bernet Galleries for a separate merchandise auction.

They made a fine job of it, and divided the stock into lots to make it attractive to dealers as well as individual customers and thereby picked up another $55,785 for the Wanamakers. Asked what he thought of the result, the Parke-Bernet auctioneer is said to have replied, "Just fair." And with the big Rovensky auction in the offing that's the way it probably looked to Parke-Bernet at the time.

With the store stripped of its stock and the merchandise both hard and soft sold and delivered there was still a vast supply of fixtures and equipment, machinery and appurtenances which had accumulated during the sixty years since John Wanamaker had acquired the business from A. T. Stewart & Co.

There had also been further reservations from the merchandise sale such as fifty tapestries, many of them wall-size, a collection of Oriental rugs, fifty-odd large paintings, some miscellaneous articles, one of the largest pipe organs in the world, and a fleet of thirty Mack trucks. For the disposition of all this the Wanamaker Company had retained the services of O. Rundle Gilbert, reputedly the greatest one-man auctioneering genius east of the Mississippi River.

This is how auctioneer Gilbert tells his story of the great sale: His first official act after getting the job was to start at the top and work his way down to the subbasement sizing up things and making a careful estimate just as he always does for an ordinary auction. He wanted to get a rough idea of how much there was to go into the sale so that he could make his plans accordingly.

He was somewhat surprised to find four restaurants, an ice cream factory, five diversified workshops devoted to construction and repair, such as a woodworking shop, a carpentry shop, and a shop for electrical repairs. He could see at a glance that the cataloguing was going to be a colossal task. He hadn't tackled anything so extensive since he auctioned off the Brooklyn *Eagle*. But with his experienced crew of eight he started the big cataloguing job one Monday morning in mid-January. They worked steadily through the rest of January and the entire month of February listing, cataloguing, segregating, and arranging, and by the time for the three-day exhibition to prospective customers and the general public the big catalogue containing some 8,000 items, many of them almost as large as an ordinary room, was ready for distribution, and so bulky that it was bound in two parts. Since the four restaurants and the five shops were scattered throughout the two buildings he had to classify the contents and bring them together for convenient handling. A charge of one dollar was made for the catalogue and an admission fee of one dollar was charged at the door to keep out triflers.

The sale opened on Monday, March 7th, and ran for eight days excluding Saturday and Sunday. Sales for the opening day were confined to the main floor and comprised the lots numbered from one to one thousand, including such articles as several miles of show cases (thirty miles in the entire store). They came in all shapes and sizes from 24 feet long and 8 feet high down to small cases for displaying watches and jewelry. There were shoe chairs with seats attached for the salesman; there was a ten-cubic-foot deep freeze for candy; item 482 was a mahogany wrapping counter followed by sixteen dittos; the items for the day covered twelve closely-printed pages in the catalogue.

On the second day they disposed of the contents of the downstairs store and the second and third floors, covering sixteen full pages of the catalogue disposing of several counters with a pegboard back, and one completely equipped golf practice range. On the third day they covered the assembled contents of four floors, occupying thirteen pages of the catalogue, selling a walnut love seat with peach upholstery, twenty life-size manikins, eleven torso forms, and one U.S. Springfield gun, dated 1863. On the fourth day they sold several lots of open-arm and "back side" chairs from the rest rooms, a stainless steel electric fudge warmer, a Hobart dishwasher 30 feet long, one box of "display legs," and seven double-faced mirrors with metal stands.

It would have been impossible to handle the crowds had they been allowed to roam all over the two large buildings. So the selling each day was restricted to a certain area in which the contents of various departments had been assembled.

And even then it was a difficult task to keep people from wandering, especially when they are inside a large building where they have previously been allowed to wander at will; then they really are hard to hold in one place. So strict precautions had been taken to keep them within the prescribed area. Pinkertons were hired to police the situation, and as prospective bidders came into the store they were ushered to certain elevators and taken to the floor where the sale was being held. But with the numerous stairways in the two buildings there were bound to be some stragglers and strays who would slip past the guards through the barricades and go exploring.

Barbed wire entanglements and a regiment of police would have been required to enforce 100 per cent privacy for the huge rambling store, but the Pinkertons were able to cope fairly well with the mavericks, and the resultant loss through pilferage was comparatively slight.

Curiously enough some of the old employees who were there to help through the auction were more troublesome about carrying things from the store than the pilferage by strangers. What these old employees mainly wanted to get away with in addition to office supplies were the typewriters and computing machines they had been using for so many years that they had really become attached to them.

There was also some switching of labels but not much. Every article in the sale had a label and the successful bidder was supposed to take his identification to the shipping department to obtain delivery, and in the confusion a few could not resist the temptation to switch a tag from a fifty-dollar chair to an eighty-dollar one. And there were some honest mistakes in the crowded shipping department by which a chair or sofa intended for New Jersey would turn up in Connecticut.

On the fifth day the auction ran into heavy goods, starting off with a thousand feet of metal shelving followed by ten hydraulic jacks, fifty National Cash Registers, one hundred Royal and Underwood typewriters with the same number of typewriter desks, and one "soyntron jogger," which is either something decidedly new, to me at least, or a misprint in the catalogue. I was present at the auction on the afternoon of the sixth day, having read in the paper that the famous Wanamaker organ would be sold that afternoon along with some other interesting items such as a large collection of wall-size tapestries, several dozen twentieth-century paintings by European artists, an outstanding collection of silk flags, some stone carvings of the heads of several famous musicians, and concluding with a large collection of executive office furniture, walnut desks, chairs, and couches, the latter no doubt being a concession to the psychiatrists.

I was especially interested in seeing how a noted auctioneer would go about selling an instrument so large that it occupied eight different rooms twenty feet by ten each, and fifteen feet high; some of them with bass pipes nearly two feet in diameter, and heaven only knows how many manuals, pedals, and stops.

The weather had been a great disappointment to me, for hardly had I reached New York before a sleet storm began. I didn't even try for a taxi and although I was able to keep under cover by means of the subway and its various underpasses, I was pretty well drenched while circling the entire Wanamaker premises to find the one of the fourteen entrances which was open to those desiring to attend the auction. When I finally found it I was admitted by a slightly superannuated doorman who brushed the sleet from my clothes with true Wanamaker solicitude.

Inside the place looked as desolate as a prison, and although

not another visitor was in sight, I could hear voices echoing
through the vast deserted building. I paid my dollar and was
admitted to the elevator, which after a loud clang from the gate,
began to move. It was no high-speed vehicle and moved like
the operator, as if tired of life.

As we passed one deserted floor after another I could still
hear the voices echoing and re-echoing from the bare walls
and empty corridors, and when I was delivered at the seventh
floor (Items 5001 to 6000) I came upon a group of workmen
moving a large counter in the direction of a freight elevator,
and heard them grunt as they struggled along such profanity
as must have offended the tender sensitivities of the Wanamaker
walls if, as people say, the walls do have ears.

The elevator man directed me to the place of the auction,
which I found momentarily silent while the auctioneer and his
two assistants seated on the rostrum were having a brief con-
ference. The audience of about one hundred people, mostly
middle-aged women, seated on folding chairs, glanced my way
as I came in and seated myself in the nearest chair, and quickly
became part of the crowd.

They had paused in selling a collection of silk flags representing principalities and regiments of Europe and the place was a
blaze of color. Few if any of these flags were recognizable, but
they were bright and glamorous and brought forth some lively
bidding when selling was resumed. They were stashed all over
the place, heaped on racks and leaning against the walls and
columns, making a brilliant display and showing to the best
advantage when unfurled and waved back and forth.

It was really a scene of great gaiety, quite unexpected at a
session of the Wanamaker auction, and especially on such a
dreary day. But it was not allowed to continue until the flags
had all been sold, for the sale of the organ had been announced
for a definite hour, and when that time came the flags were put

aside and the solemn announcement made that the great $200,000 organ would now be sold.

The auctioneer had chosen a fitting moment, for he had just finished knocking down a magnificent Spanish flag to Randolph Bullock, associate curator of Arms and Armor at the Metropolitan Museum of Art, when he cleared the decks and announced that bidding on the vast pipe organ would begin at $10,000. It was a brilliant stroke, but it fell on deaf ears, for in spite of his eloquent appeal there were no takers at that figure. Nothing, in fact, but a breath-taking silence. He knew there were bidders present and gave them ample opportunity to put in their bids; but being a keen student of crowd psychology he knew when to lower his sights and he suddenly reached for an opening bid of $5,000. But alas, there were no five-thousand-dollar bidders in the rather dowdy-looking audience sitting there in their goloshes and winter wraps in the chilly atmosphere of the almost deserted building.

The auctioneer shrewdly read the signs and took another dive. This time he called for a bid of $1,000 and immediately received a nod from Frederick D. Bouma, president of the American Institute of Organ Building of Paterson, New Jersey, who with William Tanis, a vice-president of the corporation, had come there intending to bid only if the price were "in reason."

And having received a starting bid the auctioneer now redoubled his efforts in an attempt to raise it. He filled the echoing space with his magnificent resonance, calling and cajoling in an attempt to arouse some healthy competition. He offered the great instrument as a whole or piecemeal. "You can have the fifty or the hundred horsepower motor," he said; "as many pipes as you want, or just the console."

This went on for only a short time. "One thousand I have— one thousand," he intoned. "Do I hear the two thousand?"

Finally out of the echoes came a competitor with an offer of eleven hundred. This from a representative of the Ace Equipment Company of 307 Canal Street. With a competitor in the field, the auctioneer redoubled his efforts and aroused what sounded like another competitor who interrupted proceedings by attempting to get into the contest *in absentia* by having the bids reported to him over the telephone. But before he succeeded in being anything more than a nuisance Mr. Bouma silenced him by raising the bid to $1,200. This also trumped the Ace Equipment Company and awarded to the gentleman from Paterson, New Jersey, what is said to be the most costly musical instrument in America.

The defeated contestant muttered that if successful he would have had the instrument broken up for scrap metal. But Mr. Bouma had a more constructive idea. His chief interest, he said, was in the pipes. He thought that the organ as a whole was not worth overhauling and reconstituting elsewhere. He planned to salvage about 90 per cent of the pipes, which range in size from that of a pencil to the "bombard' stop which is some eighteen inches in diameter and can thunder like the breaking of the time barrier.

In his own good time the expert explained that the quality tones are in the soft fragile pipes which extend up to about four feet in length. These are made of tin and lead, and Mr. Bouma feared a difficult job of packing since the smaller pipes bend like toothpaste tubes. He estimated that the dismantling job would take four men three weeks to accomplish. But this figure proved to be wide of the mark, for his four-man crew had the entire instrument down and off the premises within five days; and his subsequent valuation of the pipes approached $70,000 according to rumors emanating from Paterson, New Jersey, later on.

When the final day of the auction drew to its close the auctioneer's clerk punched a few knobs on her computing machine and pulled out a slip showing a total sale of $278,000. She drew a long breath and reached for her vanity case. Though the selling was over, the auction was far from completed for a large part of the merchandise was still to be delivered and paid for. Delivery of the smaller articles presented little difficulty to the auctioneer, but the removal of such utilitarian items as refrigerators, 30-foot dishwashers (item 3368), and other appliances still attached to the buildings presented a more serious problem, especially since the City of New York has hundreds of regulations which tell you what you can and cannot do. The plumber who puts in your appliance may not be allowed to take it out, and the outside man who is to take it away may not be permitted to come in and get it.

The wisdom of a Solomon is needed to settle all these inconsistencies without arousing hard feelings, and the auctioneer and his crew must be not only experts at soothing ruffled feathers but jacks-of-all-trades in the removal, dismemberment, packing and loading of anything that is likely to go under the hammer.

And then there are always last-moment discoveries which can become a serious nuisance, such as the sixty display tables found in a dark corner of a subbasement of Wanamaker's. They were angrily hauled out by the leg and offered to anybody, including passers-by, for a dollar apiece though worth five or six dollars. At first nobody wanted them, for what can you do on a city street with a display table on your hands? The bus won't let you on with even a pair of skis, and a taxi couldn't possibly carry anything as bulky as a display table.

What happened in this case was that an enterprising trucking concern from the country which had been delivering produce in the city bought the whole lot and peddled them to the inhabitants of Southern New Jersey at a good profit. And it was not until the final piece of the last appliance had been detached from the freehold and removed from the building, when all the doors had been closed and barred, and the great bronze keys had been turned in the locks and surrendered to the new owners that the famous John Wanamaker store at Broadway and Ninth Street passed out of the New York scene.

For a time the entire property remained vacant before the southernmost unit was remodeled to accommodate various enterprises, and more than a year passed before the new management had begun the demolition of the northerly unit to make way for a large apartment house development, when a fire broke out in the partially demolished building which raged out of control for nearly four days and gave New York City one of its most spectacular conflagrations in a hundred years.

As the fire raged on day after day, being retarded in one place only to break out in another, great crowds of sightseers gathered from all parts of the metropolitan area and from the surrounding towns as well. Parents brought their children from as far away as Albany and New Haven to see the holocaust, and the police had great difficulty in maintaining their fire lines against the great pressure of closely-packed crowds trying to edge their way forward to get a better view of the disaster.

All surface traffic had been blocked from the area since the initial alarm, and it was not long before subway traffic was discontinued for fear of collapse from above, especially after the tubes had become flooded to the ceiling with the tons of water being pumped into the burning building from all sides.

However, Grace Church, being just beyond the fire lines, continued to hold its regular services during the holocaust despite the sirens, the bellowing of the loud speakers, and the other din and confusion going on just outside the stained glass windows. And New York's "Finest," with their usual efficiency, continuously maintained an open passage for the entry and exit of churchgoers, though one of the regulars on the Wanamaker beat remarked afterward that he never realized before that the church had so many members—or so many meetings.

A quarter of a million dollars worth of building materials were destroyed, and a scandal was threatened over the gross negligence of the night watchman in failing for several hours after he had first smelled the smoke to give the alarm. However, the blame was finally laid to the numerous bums who were known to have been sleeping in the partially demolished building.

And it eventually came to pass in the wide-open spaces of Westchester where the suburbanite swings off the Sawmill River route and into the Cross-County Parkway, a proud new Wanamaker's has arisen in all its glory, named for its illustrious ancestor—John.

CHAPTER TWENTY

OVER THE TOP

THE GREAT AUCTION HOUSES OF NEW YORK, LONDON, AND PARIS all experienced an unprecedented boom in the year 1957. So far as New York was concerned, the lush times were inaugurated in January with a series of auctions disposing of the vast collections of jewels, tapestries, porcelains, and other works of art belonging to the estate of the late Mae Caldwell Manwaring Plant Hayward Rovensky in the mellow splendor of the Parke-Bernet Galleries on upper Madison Avenue.

Eleven sessions were required to dispose of the vast Rovensky holdings, which at the conclusion of the sale had reached a total sales value of $2,438,980, thereby breaking the American record of the Elbert H. Gary sale which had stood unchallenged since 1928.

Sale of the jewelry alone fractured another American record, realizing under the hammer the very considerable amount of $1,122,865, being the first one-day jewelry auction in America to exceed the sum of one million dollars. The most fabulous piece among the jewels was the 213.10-carat necklace consisting of ninety-four diamonds, which had been presented to Mrs. Rovensky in 1917 by Commodore Morton Plant, the second of her four husbands.

At a meeting of the executors of her estate held a few days before the sale it was decided that the opening bid for the necklace should be placed at $350,000. This sounds like a rather large amount, as the minimum bid for a bauble to hang around a woman's neck, but it is less than half the $750,000 paid for it in 1917 when diamonds were worth somewhat less than they are today.

Also featured in the sale were two oriental pearl necklaces received in a unique deal with Cartier's for the exchange of the town house on Fifth Avenue which has ever since remained the business address of the jewelers. One is inclined to wonder whether any of these necklaces was ever worn outside the confines of a safe-deposit stronghold, and if so, when and where, and how many special police were assembled as a bodyguard—and what was the occasion.

But to return to the 23rd of January—the incredible diamond necklace, after having been exhibited draped over a black velvet form, passed under the hammer at the unbelievable price of $385,000, bought by one Julius Furst of 32 West Forty-seventh Street, thereby establishing a new American record of the highest price paid for a single item at auction. It thus exceeds by a round $10,000 a record which had stood since May, 1929, when a painting of the Crucifixion by Piero della Francesca, an Italian artist, was sold by auction from the Carl W. Hamilton collection.

Harry Winston, a New York jeweler, had the honor of bidding on the peerless Rovensky necklace but was easily outdistanced by Mr. Furst who afterward modestly explained that his bidding was in consultation with a group of jewelers, and predicted that he would sell the necklace at a substantial profit before leaving the galleries.

If any such turnover was negotiated it most certainly was not publicized. But secrecy in such matters is not unusual, for not only do jewel operators shrink from having the public know too much about their business, but since the Brink episode in Boston they have not felt quite so secure about the time locks and the burglarproof arrangements as they formerly did.

The two handsome pearl necklaces also went under the hammer that same day, but after the big moment everything else seemed like anticlimax. One brought $90,000, and the other the more modest sum of $61,000 from a European buyer who, for reasons best known to himself, slipped away without giving his name to the papers. Harry Winston tried again on the pearl necklaces but lost, though he later succeeded with a 30-carat diamond ring for which he bid $116,000.

As far as was made known to the public, only one serious loss occurred during the succession of auctions and periods of inspection, and it was on one of the inspection days that a diamond bar pin valued at $20,000 mysteriously disappeared despite the watchfulness of Pinkerton operatives as well as an army of clerks accustomed to showing costly items to a miscellaneous public assemblage. Of course there were many pieces on display at the time as well as drifting crowds of visitors examining and inspecting them, and it was all in a day's work when a well-dressed gentleman asked one of the clerks if he might examine the bar pin more closely.

There was nothing unusual about the request. Prospective buyers almost invariably want to handle and examine closely a jewel that is intended for his beloved one, and especially a very handsome pearl and diamond pin which might easily bring more than its appraised value when offered in an auction at which the prices had been running wild, the place filled with wealthy and discriminating purchasers who would be present on the day of sale. The woman clerk, who was only too glad to have a prospective customer show an interest in a fairly expensive piece, took the bar pin from the showcase and laid it on top at the exact moment when a lady customer at the farther end of the showcase created a slight disturbance by demanding

impatiently to be shown another article as if she had been waiting some time for attention and was very much annoyed. She
was only a few steps away, and the clerk, not wishing to add
to the annoyance of a customer, quickly stepped over to wait
on her while the gentleman was examining the bar pin. The
clerk was delayed there for only a moment or two and when
she started to return to the gentleman customer she was
astonished to find that he had disappeared—and to her horror
the bar pin had disappeared with him—and when she turned
back to look for the lady customer, she too was gone.

After assuring herself that the bar pin really was gone, she
rushed to the nearest Pinkerton with her heart beating wildly
and reported what had happened. He quickly spread the alarm,
but the two thieves had made their escape. The police, who
were summoned immediately upon the discovery of the loss,
were unable to find any clue to the perpetrator of the theft or
to unearth any description, indicating that a jewel thief known
to the police had slipped into town without their knowledge.
They talked learnedly about the methods in such an operation
where two crooks played into each other's hand, but no arrests
were made and the bar pin was never recovered. Luckily it
was insured.

Officials of the Galleries were jubilant over the high prices
which had outstripped the advance appraisal by more than 30
per cent and one of them was quoted as saying that it's easier to
sell a twelve-thousand-dollar article for fifteen thousand dollars
than a two-hundred-dollar article for two hundred dollars. An
ordinary sale is something of a bargain sale; however, it doesn't
matter to the rich that they pay a few thousand dollars more—
or less—for an object if they really want it.

Part I Art, which comprised rare porcelains, silver, tapestries
and rugs as well as fine English and French furniture was sold
on January 15 to 19 inclusive for $1,160,070. Among the out-
standing prices obtained were $50,000 for the celebrated Ash-

burnham gilded silver toilet service by Benjamin Pyne, 1719; three Royal Beauvais tapestries depicting scenes from Moliere's plays brought $37,500, $27,000, and $18,000 respectively; $69,000 for a pair of paintings by François Boucher; $12,000 for a Chelsea tureen in the form of a rabbit, purchased by the Antique Porcelain Company Limited of London, who also purchased a Louis XV gold snuff box set with diamonds for $17,000, and a pair of Meissen porcelain figures of woodpeckers by J. J. Kändler for $19,000; a Louis XIV Savonnerie floral carpet went for $33,500.

Part II of the art property, mainly from the Rovensky Newport residence, Clarenden Court, went under the hammer on January 24, 25, and 26 for a total of $204,340. In this sale, a Chelsea tureen in the form of a pair of pigeons brought $10,500; a pair of Bow bird-group candlesticks, $8,800, both bought by the Antique Porcelain Company, Limited; and a silver bowl by Paul Lamerie, $5,250.

Part I Art was exhibited at the 1051 Fifth Avenue mansion where it had been domiciled since 1917, for two days preceding the regular showing at Parke-Bernet, for the benefit of Hungarian relief, attracting more than 6,000 visitors. At the galleries over 30,000 people witnessed the four-part exhibition and sale, the peaks coming January 16, 18, and 19 when the paintings were auctioned and the major works of art were sold. However, it was on Wednesday afternoon, January 23, when the largest throng filled the salesroom. Audiences included a number of British and French antiquarians who had flown to New York especially for the sale, notables of the American art world, and people prominent in society and theatrical circles.

The fourth and final part, the library, went under the hammer January 29 and 30 for a total of $51,705. Some of the outstanding prices were $3,100 for a first edition of La Fontaine; a magnificent memento of Lord Nelson and Lady Hamilton in superb binding with colored portrait miniatures of the pair, including medals commemorating the victory and a significant military order written by him during the campaign brought $2,800. Included with all this was a lock of Nelson's hair and threads from the sash he wore at the Battle of Trafalgar when he was slain. Another Nelson item was a letter written by Lady Hamilton complaining of her treatment by the government after Nelson's death.

As a rule all gallery estimates are predicated on quality and rarity of objects, on previous auction prices for comparable items, and in the case of a famous collection, on its "name" value. But these rules proved unreliable in the Rovensky sale, for prices went soaring from the opening bids. A Savonnerie carpet appraised to sell at $15,000 went for $33,500; a 30-carat diamond ring appraised at $100,000 brought $116,000; and a foreign buyer paid $82,500 for three Royal Beauvais tapestries which had been appraised at a top of $45,000. The same purchaser also bought a celebrated George I silver toilet service for $50,000 and two oriental pearl necklaces for $151,000, both far above appraisal valuation.

Whether this was caused by the lush prosperity of the times, or the foresightedness of people about getting their wealth invested in property more stable than money or securities during the unpredictable tactics of the Soviets would be hard to say with any certainty; but the success of the Rovensky dispersal was undeniably epoch-making.

What it was, however, which inspired Mrs. Rovensky to gather about her such a vast collection of art and beauty is an even more puzzling question. Just the responsibility of protecting and caring for such a collection of irreplaceable treasure must have been staggering as well as costly, though cost does not seem to have been a consideration in her case. That Mr. Leslie Hyam, President of Parke-Bernet, has been doing some

constructive thinking along kindred lines is shown by the following comments taken from his foreword in one of the gallery
catalogues of the Rovensky sales:

"It is not my purpose here to set forth in full the
nature and extent of Mrs. Rovensky's collections; nor,
on the other hand, to attempt a social history, however
abbreviated, of an age that is conceded on all sides to
be past. What is most interesting—at least to the writer
—is something else. It is the nature of the impulse that
brought together, for example, under one roof the
Oudry Molière tapestries, the Spartan silver of Charles
II and the sculptural silver of Paul Lamerie; Chelsea
porcelain and the sophisticated and very different
Meissen of Kändler; Elizabethan-Carolean oak and
the delicacies of the Age of Satinwood; simplicity and
perfection in the seat furniture of Louis Quinze; the
long galaxy of portraits, from the harsh glitter of Con-
rad Faber and the serenity of del Sarto to Romney's
and Lawrence's dashing patricians; Mrs. Rovensky's
two favorite Boucher pastorales; the gold, the coral
and the jade; and a collection of table porcelains staggering in quantity and quality.

"What seems to emerge . . . may be put this way:
that here was someone who believed with great sin-
cerity that the social order was immutably secure;
that the meaning of wealth, as with the merchant
princes of the Renaissance, was that it should be
translated into an environment of beauty and dignity,
as its proper appanages; and that once the eye was
trained to the pursuit, the appeal of great craftsman-
ship was irresistible, and its ownership a justification
of one's position. This point of view appears in

Morgan, Widener, Hearst, Walters and others of the omnivorous collectors of the first rank. It is suffused with the glow of American pragmatism, which was also the pragmatism of the Fuggers and the Medici."

The ink was hardly dry on the records of the Rovensky auctions when, on February 28 of this gala year, the art world was thrilled by a dispatch to the New York papers from San Moritz clearing up the mystery surrounding the rumored sale of the famous Edward G. Robinson collection of the French Impressionists. The message had come from Stavros Spyros Niarchos, shipping tycoon and one of the richest men in the modern world, letting it be known that he was the individual for whom Knoedler & Company had bought some fifty-eight paintings and a bronze from the Robinson collection for something over three million dollars.

It was well known in California that the collection would eventually have to go, for there had been a divorce in the Robinson family, and a valuable collection of pictures is something that cannot be divided up like a bank account or a bundle of stocks and bonds, or even a few thousand acres of oil-bearing lands, for California is a joint-property state and is not a good place in which to reside if a couple is planning a divorce, especially when the husband has spent the best years of his life amassing a collection of pictures, all of which are his favorites.

However, the climate of California is conducive to divorce, especially among those belonging to the Hollywood stardom, and the laws of the state are strict and impartial about the equal division of community property; and when the family assets are of such a nature as to be physically incapable of an equal division in kind, the law steps in and directs an equal division of the cash the property will bring on a sale.

Such was the situation in the case of Robinson vs. Robinson. It may sound simple enough, but where the bulk of the property consists of objects without a fixed or assessable value, and of a price that may fluctuate by many thousands of dollars as often as the object changes hands, the problem presented is one that might well have puzzled King Solomon himself.

In this case the wife had a distinct advantage. Not being a collector, she presumably cared less for the pictures than her husband who was a born collector and who had spent a fortune in time and money acquiring the pictures one by one as the opportunity was presented. It is said that as a lad he was an ardent collector of cigar bands. Whatever became of them is immaterial, and how it happened that he turned to paintings instead of postage stamps is known only to himself.

Robinson was a top-notch actor of hard-boiled characters and had reached the thousand-a-week plateau before he became known to the big auction galleries as an occasional buyer of French Moderns. It was not until after his smashing success in *Little Caesar* when his movie salary was boosted to seven thousand a week that he began to acquire some of the finest works of the Impressionists and post-Impressionists and was soon recognized by the authorities as a real connoisseur.

Among his canvases were some of the finest of Corot, Cézanne, Renoir, Matisse, van Gogh, Degas, Gauguin, and nearly all the master painters that France has produced in the last half century.

After negotiations lasting some six months, during which Robinson was represented by one negotiator, his wife by another, and Niarchos by a third, Knoedler succeeded in closing a deal by the terms of which the collection was sold to Niarchos with a privilege to Robinson of buying back some fourteen of the canvases at an estimated price of $500,000; and at the final settlement the value of the works acquired by Niarchos has simmered down to about $2,500,000. And somewhere in the deal there must have been a commission to Knoedler of more than $250,000 which is about the way such things go.

Niarchos already was owner of a prized El Greco for which he had paid $400,000. If only he had come into his money a few years earlier, what a glorious time he and Duveen could have had covering the walls of his town houses in Paris and Athens, his penthouses in New York and London, and his chateau on the French Riviera with some of the finest art of the world at the spectacular Duveen prices.

While Mr. Niarchos has made no announcement whether any of the pictures purchased in the Robinson deal will be removed from this country, rumors have been going about in art circles that they will be hung at least temporarily in his Manhattan penthouse. Only four months after the Robinson purchase Mr. Niarchos was again on the firing line in a sensational auction at the spectacular Galerie Charpentier in Paris for the sale of the noted Margaret Biddle collection of forty-five French canvases which had been collected with rare discrimination during her many years of residence in rue Las Casas where she was known as a very distinguished and very wealthy American Francophile.

By the time of the Biddle sale Niarchos' purchase of the Robinson collection was well known to connoisseurs on both continents, and when he was seen at the Biddle auction it was immediately suspected by the wiseacres that he was in quest of the Gauguin "Still Life with Apples," and possibly some of the other highly desirable gems in the distinguished Biddle collection. But as the crowd of some two thousand sat sweltering in the heat of the June day a whisper went through the crowd that Mr. Basil Goulandris, another shipping magnate of Greek origin, had put in an appearance quite obviously for the same purpose, since it was known that he was interested in the French Moderns and had already acquired a famous El Greco and a superb Cézanne at what might be considered Duveen prices.

Both these Greek gentlemen were almost indecently wealthy, and were supposedly business rivals. So an exciting contest was almost unavoidable.

Just the name of Biddle had brought out a good sampling of French society folk. In spite of the intense heat there was a Rothschild present and a Talleyrand, for instance. Fine auctions such as this invariably bring out fine ladies in Paris who try to show an interest in the arts as well as in fashions; and there they sat perspiring freely but politely as they waited for the *chef d'oeuvre* to go up on the easel.

When finally the Gauguin canvas went up for display there was only a smattering of applause, as if the audience were more excited over the contest than they were over the picture itself. Everybody was agreed that the picture was good, but how great it really was would be determined by the price. None of the experts expected it to go beyond thirty or forty million francs, and the opening bid of twenty million had them nodding their heads in agreement; but when it quickly passed forty-five million and went hurtling on at a million francs a bid they were obviously nonplussed.

Indeed, by this time the bids were coming so rapidly that one could hardly be sure who was doing the bidding and which bidder was in the lead, though everybody felt sure that it was one or the other of the Greeks, even though the bids were coming from all directions. However, when the bid reached one hundred million francs there was a breathing spell for everybody when the entire audience leaped to their feet with excitement and applause. But as soon as they were quieted down the bidding was resumed at a lesser pace, and when it had reached one hundred and four million francs the hammer descended and the name of the buyer was given as Basil Peter Goulandris of the Orion Shipping Company of New York. The figure was presumably the highest ever paid for a modern painting.

Gauguin himself did not price it so highly, for when he
finished the painting in 1901 he sold it to Ambroise Vollard, an
art merchant, for two hundred francs, worth at the time about
forty dollars, with Vollard complaining that Gauguin had
robbed him—even at that price. A trainload of apples—real
apples—could be bought for the Biddle price which, figured in
dollars, would come to about two hundred and ninety-seven
thousand, to be exact $297,142.

The home of Margaret Thompson Biddle, who died in 1956,
had long been an intellectual and artistic center, and the paintings were put on sale by her children to raise money for the
charity fund which bears her name. But France, like England,
has been touchy of late about having art treasures taken out of
the country, and prior to the opening of the sale there must
have been a pretty piece of diplomatic maneuvering, for when
at the sale Maurice Rheims, the auctioneer, read to the assemblage a cablegram presumably just received from the Biddle
family in America announcing the presentation of Renoir's
splendid canvas, "The Casbah," to the Louvre, an announcement was made on behalf of the French Government con-
senting to the removal of the paintings in the Biddle sale beyond
the French frontiers, a bit of back-scratching much appreciated
by Americans and other foreigners in the audience.

Prices had been high from the beginning of the sale. Such
warming-up items as a Ribers brought 3,200,000 francs, and
a Boudin went soaring up over 13,000,000. A Gauguin landscape brought 14,000,000 francs, his still life without any apples
touched 35,000,000, and four Renoir canvases brought more
than 100,000,000.

There were times at the auction when the excitement rose
to such a pitch that some impulsive females in the audience
couldn't help raising their hands although they had no real
intention of bidding, and several times the usually unruffled
auctioneer was compelled to go back and recapitulate before

he could be sure who had the right of way, so great was the confusion.

This Biddle sale was one of the largest the rue de Faubourg St. Honoré had seen in years. It comprised about one hundred paintings including forty-four from the Biddle estate which withheld some twenty paintings for private sale. The total intake from the auction was nearly half a billion francs of which the Biddle collection accounted for about three hundred five million, all of which will go to the Margaret Thompson Biddle Foundation for medical research, as was announced at the auction.

The famous Biddle silver-gilt table service with its massive platters, plates, serving dishes, and table settings did not appear at the auction, for it had been a specific bequest under her will to the United States Government for use at the White House.

Summing up these goings-on the magazine *Life*, without waiting for the end of the year, made the following comment:

> "Such soaring prices have left both art dealers and auctioneers gasping. But avid art buyers who at auctions in the past season have spent more than $9 million in New York City, $12 million in London and $10 million in Paris, continue to boost the boom and make canvas the most expensive material in the world."

These things had been happening when the year was only half gone, and by the time the frost was on the pumpkin a gigantic sale of sixty-five paintings from the magnificent collection of French Moderns left by the late George Lurcy was being heralded for the Parke-Bernet Galleries for the first week in November. Coming as it did after the Rovensky sale, the Robinson affair, the excitement in Paris over the "Still Life with Apples," and the astonishing Weinberg sale at Sotheby's in which the initial use of television at a sale of the fine arts

was inaugurated—the Lurcy management was so overwhelmed
with applications for tickets that the supply was exhausted
almost within hours of the time when the announcement of
the sale was made. The probability is that Madison Square
Garden would not have been large enough to accommodate
all the patrons of the arts who would have liked to attend. But
the human eye can distinguish a painting to advantage for only
a limited distance and the Parke-Bernet management wisely
confined the sale to their own premises, using all the available
rooms with the aid of television and an open circuit telephone
by which bids made in one room could be registered by the
auctioneer in another.

The Thursday night opening was an affair of white ties and
tails, and this time it was Renoir instead of Gauguin who walked
off with the top money for his "La Serre," a simple garden scene
with a rustic greenhouse which went to Henry Ford II for
an even $200,000. No telling what figure might have been
reached if only apples had been in season. But Gauguin was not
far behind, for his "Mau Taporo," a sixty-five-year-old painting of a Tahitian woman, a tree, and a horse, was runner-up at
$180,000 and was bought by Alex Goulandris (brother of
Basil Goulandris who purchased the fabulous Gauguin still
life), the Greek shipping magnate, who also purchased a Bon-
nard "Still Life with Cat" for $70,000.

The bidders were really on a buying spree. Every picture
that went up on the easel started a battle and in every case far
exceeded its estimated value. The Renoir garden scene which
hit the top surmounted the appraised value by $60,000 and a
café scene by Toulouse-Lautrec beat the appraisal by $35,000.
Even a charcoal drawing by Picasso which went for $9,000
was about a thousand dollars over the estimate. The wives of
the shipping magnates were present on this august occasion,
though so far as is known they did no actual bidding. However,
Mrs. David Rockefeller, who was there with her husband,

bought a beach scene by Signac for $31,000. But in general it was difficult to tell who was bidding and for whom, for many of the buyers were represented by agents, some of whom were bidding for several different clients. Edward G. Robinson, who was present, bought a Derain for $5,500 and a Braque for about twelve thousand through an agent.

The total for the opening night came to $1,708,550 again topping the Elbert H. Gary record of 1928 which had already been beaten earlier in the year by the Rovensky sale.

On the afternoon following the opening night came the second session of the Lurcy sale including the modern prints, paintings and drawings, table porcelain and glass, silver and plated wear, and also French furniture and objects of art; the third and last session held Saturday afternoon included porcelains, Majolica, old silver, sculptures, rugs, and miscellaneous objects of art, these two sessions adding another half million of proceeds, bringing the total receipts of the Lurcy sale up to $2,221,355.

This sum added to the nine million dollar total for New York City mentioned in the preceding *Life* magazine compilation brings the New York total dangerously near the leading position ascribed to London. All of which proves very little except that the moneyed people in Europe and America invested a tremendous amount of their surplus funds in works of art during the year 1957.

Can it be that the world is coming to believe that the picture frame makes a better strongbox for the wealth of mankind than the bank vault? Or does it merely signify that more and more of the beautiful things of the world are headed for the museum where the value can no longer be represented by the fluctuation of dollars and cents?

EPILOGUE

Soon after starting this book it occurred to me that it might be useful or at least desirable to know how many auctioneers we have in this country and, if possible, how much business they are transacting annually. So I wrote to the Census Bureau in Washington thinking that they would, of course, be able to furnish me with the information. They responded politely in the negative and suggested that I contact some of the other Washington bureaus, such as the National Production Authority of the Department of Commerce, or the Marketing Service of the United States Department of Agriculture, among others.

I wrote to all they had mentioned, receiving very prompt and courteous attention, but very little of the information I desired. Several of them sent samples of their folders and pamphlets, probably to convince me that they had nothing to do with auctions or auctioneers, but which showed a willing spirit and a desire to help. One of the most impressive of these "mail-outs" as I believe they are called, came from the Department of Agriculture and purported to contain a list of all available publications of the Department compiled by Eleanor W. Clay, Division of Publications, Office of Information, superseding Miscellaneous Publication 60, for sale by the Superintendent of Documents, U.S. Printing office, issued 1954, price forty-five cents paper-bound.

This looked so impressive that I felt sure it must contain something about auctions, and after going carefully through 123 closely-printed pages I found under Farmer Cooperative Service a very brief mention of "Terminal Fruit Auctions as marketing agents for farmer cooperatives," issued in 1938. There was still another entry which mentioned "cooperative shipping point auctions for fruits and vegetables," issued in 1951.

There were thousands of other tempting bulletins mentioned in the pamphlet at reasonable prices running from five cents to one dollar, but since they had nothing to do with auctions I had to forego them all.

By this time I was all through trying to get information from any of the government bureaus, and I sat down and wrote a letter to one of our senators in Washington. Almost by return mail I received a letter from the director of the Legislative Reference Service of the Library of Congress written at the request of the senator, informing me that it was reported in the Census of Business for 1948 (ten years before) that there were 670 auctioneers' establishments with receipts totaling $14,535,000 for that year.

As service that was excellent, though as news it was almost an antique. However, I have read in a recent *Newsweek* magazine that there are now at least 20,000 auctioneers at work across the country—perhaps as many as 35,000; and at the latest government count there were over 18,000 wholesale auction houses doing better than a three billion dollar a year business, while some retail houses are pocketing a commission of over twenty-two million a year.

This means that only one tenth of the auction houses in our country are doing a business of $3,022,000,000 in a single year. When—if ever—the remaining 90 per cent of our auctioneers are heard from their totals will no doubt look like the astronomical calculations of a spaceship.

Never before have the great auction galleries in the big cities wallowed in such prosperity as during the present era. They have broken every conceivable record of modern times for the total intake of auctions and top prices for individual items in the field of art. Then too, the rush for tickets when a notable auction is announced is not unlike the annual battle for World Series tickets, or cards for the Inaugural Ball. And an evening auction at one of the large galleries brings out as much mink and as many diamond necklaces and bared shoulders as the opera or a debutantes' ball.

All the noted collectors are there either in person or by proxy. They sit quietly in the audience, program and pencil in hand, bidding with the flick of a finger such prices as would have made the great Duveen gasp with envy; while the curiosity seekers in the balcony, who are there largely for thrills, sometimes forget where they are and come to their feet with applause and cheering reminiscent of the bleachers at a ball game.

The country auctions, of course, are conducted on an entirely different level. Today almost everybody in the country is making a collection of something. It may be pewter if one is opulent, or buttons or glass slippers if one is a bit on the rocks. The big old country houses with attics and lofts are catchalls for the preservation of relics for future generations, and anything from a sofa to a thimble is likely to be tucked away in a dark corner under an angle of the roof for a hundred years or more before being dragged out of obscurity for an auction sale at which an old and battered chair may find itself in a spirited contest between a determined housewife who feels sure that it would just fit grandpa, and a city dealer who has recognized it as an old Dutch bedchair—very scarce and costly, and almost exactly like the one he has seen at the Cooper Institute in New York.

The why and wherefore of the immense popularity of the

auction in both city and country at the present time is some-what enigmatic. The prevalence of the motorcar and the vast improvement of the country roads have undoubtedly enlarged the territory of the urban buyers, especially the collectors who will go many miles for even a slim chance to acquire a single item, and one never can tell what antique treasures may come out of one of these old country attics—such as the recently dis-covered rarity known as the hornbook.

Then too, the inborn gambling spirit may have something to do with the wide appeal of the auction and the teasing un-certainty that keeps the bidding alive; but the desire to win is as strong in the musty tent of the country auction as in the most fastidious and sophisticated auditorium of a city gallery, and the insistent urgency of the ringing words, "Going once—going twice—going third and last call!" is usually the same whether you are buying a cow or a Corot. Then with the crash of the hammer the bargain is sealed.

And if anyone is worried about a drying up of sources of supply, where but in the American back country could one find the sign, which I saw recently in a little town down in Maine, that reads:

ANTIQUES

Bought, Sold, & Made to Order